Popular Culture Review
Volume 26, No. 2
Summer 2015

From the Editor's Desk

We have wonderful news. In a few weeks, all twenty-seven years of *Popular Culture Review* will be available through Westphalia Press with whom we have just joined forces for printing and distribution. This will both increase our circulation and provide a permanent archive. Each volume will retain its format and be separately bound. After the volumes appear in print, they will also be submitted for publication in Amazon's Kindle e-book program.

In this issue Erika Engstrom and Colby Miyose discuss a new masculinity in Korean Soap Opera, while Lorna Gibb tackles writing about ghosts and blurring the lines between biography and fiction. Kristin Barton and Josh Bates examine the unfortunate homogenous influence *American Idol* exerts on musical artistry, while Todd Giles discusses the more salubrious use of Benjamin Britten's Theme and Variation in Wes Anderson's *Moonrise Kingdom*. Class and artistic identity lie at the heart of Philip Castille's analysis of Jack London's *Martin Eden* in "The Call of the Colonial." Lastly Patricia and William Kirtley argue that comics and popular culture do belong in the classroom. Four book reviews provide hints for future readings.

Remember that we are the journal of the Far West Popular and American Culture Associations without whom *PCR* would not exist. Our 28th annual meeting is scheduled from February 26 -28, 2016 at the Palace Station Hotel in Las Vegas. Our meetings are attended by people from around the world and are known for their friendliness and the quality of intellectual exchange. I am accepting abstracts now at felicia.campbell@unlv.edu.

Felicia Campbell

Boys Over Flowers:
Korean Soap Opera and the
Blossoming of a New Masculinity

Colby Miyose[A] and Erika Engstrom[A]

When it premiered on South Korean television in 2009, the Korean drama (or "K-drama") Boys Over Flowers became a ratings sensation, mostly among females between their mid-teens to thirties (AGB Neilsen Media Research, n.d.). Originally a Japanese *manga* (comic book), the Korean television version became the third iteration of the story of teenage love and romance, following Taiwanese and Japanese television versions. Boys Over Flowers serves as one of the major starting influences of the *kkonminam* or "flower boy" craze (Jung, 2010). In its literal translation *kkot* means "flower," while *minam* means "handsome man." Merged together, these terms create "flower boy" (Maliangkay, 2010). Qualities of the *kkonminam* are frequently linked to characters in Japanese *manga* stories of teenage schoolgirls and their romantic relationships with their *bishonen* ("beautiful boy") boyfriends (Jung, 2010). Extending beyond just Korea, one can find evidence of a strong reception of the "flower boy" craze globally via websites such as YouTube, ViiKii, and Dramabean (Jung, 2010).

Set at the fictional prestigious Shinhwa High School, a sort of "Harvard" of South Korea for the country's richest and most elite children, Boys Over Flowers follows the trials and tribulations a clique of boys who "rule the school" and the young working-class girl named Jan Di who becomes a transforming force in their lives. The narrative of Boys Over Flowers centers on the themes of love and friendship as experienced by Jan Di, her best friend, and the group of four Shinwa male students known as the "F4," or Flower 4 (Boys Over Flowers, n.d.). Jung (2010) noted that Boys Over Flowers is a retelling of the classic fairy tale Cinderella, with the addition of a love triangle and emphasis on materialism.

Regarding the meaning of the phrase "boys over flowers," the original Japanese title, Hana Yori Dango, literally translates as "dumplings rather than [over] flowers" (Jung, 2010), a Japanese proverb inspired by families going to festivals that celebrated *Hanami*, the viewing of cherry blossom flowers, when they enjoyed eating sweet dumplings more than viewing the blossoming of the cherry trees (Sosnoski, 1996). In a figurative sense, *hana yori dango* means that one should enjoy and aspire to attain tangible happiness rather

---

[A] University of Nevada, Las Vegas

than aesthetics (Jung, 2010). From this idea, the creator of the *manga* series replaced the literal meaning of the word *dango* from "dumplings" to mean "boy," resulting in the adage that women should choose men for their character rather than for their looks (Jung, 2010).

This study investigates how the popular Korean version of *Boys Over Flowers* offers portrayals of both hegemonic and counterhegemonic masculinity, and how this particular mass media text treats and redefines culturally held notions of masculinity within the Korean culture (though still connected through a historically common original culture prior to the separation into north and south, "Korea" hereafter refers to South Korea). A textual analysis identifies overarching themes that appear in characters' storylines and portrayals, which, taken together, evidences how this K-drama offers a new version of masculinity that challenges traditional masculinity and recasts the "ideal guy" for its mostly female audience.

Hegemonic Masculinity in Korean Culture

Garde (2003) suggests that Western hegemonic masculinity encompasses four dominant norms featuring masculinity: power, opposition toward femininity, domination and objectification of nature, and the avoidance of emotion. Major similarities emerge when comparing hegemonic masculinities of Western societies to South Korean society, especially regarding heteronormativity and patriarchal ideology. For example, Moon (2002) noted that Confucian tradition, militarization, and compressed industrialization serve as the bases for Korean notions of masculinity. The patriarchal ideologies of Confucianism can be traced to the *Sam-Kang-Oh-Ryun* (the three Fundamental and Five Moral Laws), which has influenced Korean socio-political society for most of the country's history (Kim & Hahn, 2006); it maintains a patriarchal base of power for both the state and the family. Confucian patriarchy later transformed into modern industrialized patriarchy, which adopted the normative Western dichotomy of gender roles into its dominant gender ideology, with South Korea's mandatory military service (due to the continued confrontation between North and South Korea), adding another element of Korean hegemonic masculinity, (Moon, 2002).

Moon (2002) further suggested that gender dichotomy in Korea can be traced to the idea of *seonbi* (the term for a Confucian scholar seeking wisdom) masculinity, from the Joseon dynasty of 1392-1910 CE. *Seonbi* masculinity dictates that men are not to engage in daily domestic labor, which, though absolutely necessary for the maintenance of society, is degrading and should be performed by women (Moon, 2002). Though blatantly sexist, *seonbi* masculinity is still regarded as an ideal model of Korean masculinity, because it represents traditional values such as virtue, faithfulness, and loyalty (Geum, 2000).

3

Counterhegemonic Masculinity:
The Budding of the *Kkonminam*

Media depictions of masculinity may be reflecting the transforming gender norms that are occurring throughout various cultures, such as the introduction of the "new man" (Frederick, 2006). The "new man" persona forwards a revised masculinity that promotes traits such as being sensitive, expressive, and domestically savvy (Beyon, 2002). The metrosexual serves as another version of new masculinity; it refers to the image-conscious man who spends a considerable amount of time and resources on his appearance and lifestyle (Pompper, 2010). According to Aldrich (2004), the metrosexual is a heterosexual who is in touch with his feminine side, though others may consider him to be gay or bisexual. Merging these perspectives on masculine scripts together creates the overarching notion of "millennium masculinity," whose major features include: (a) the pursuit of good health and appearance; (b) the absence of being a father; (c) the disassociation from violent behaviors; and (d) a personality consisting of vulnerability and incompetence (Beyon, 2002). The "new man" persona thus increasingly depends on matters of style and self-presentation, diverging from the traditional models of masculinity centered on reputation and work.

The characteristics of the "flower boy" reflect somewhat the "millennium masculinity" in Western societies. The requisite attributes of a *kkonminam* are: (a) girl-like pretty looks, (b) toned and hairless body, (c) a vulnerable heart, and (d) an inconsiderate and immature personality (Jung, 2010). The emergence of *kkonminam* parallels the changing socio-political atmosphere in South Korea following an economic downturn related to the International Monetary Fund (see Cho, 2013) and the subsequent loss of women in the Korean workforce due to layoffs. Decades of significant gender inequality in the workplace, combined with the patriarchal idea that women should be secondary to men, contributed to the emergence of a softer male image (Maliangkay, 2010). This counter-hegemonic version of masculinity forwards the image of a more androgynous male, and has the potential to make the opposite sex (women) look more powerful, bringing both sexes closer to a level of egalitarianism (Maliangkay, 2010).

The *kkonminam* image began its popularity in the Korean entertainment industry in the late 1990s, with television commercials, dramas, and billboard advertisements featuring pretty boys with smooth skin, silky hair, and a feminine demeanor (Jung, 2010). This new vision of masculinity soon began to displace the hegemonic notion of macho, aggressive masculinity, with the Korean "tough guy" look strongly contested by the "flower boy" trend (Jung, 2010). The *kkonminam* syndrome has developed not because of males having become more feminized, but as a consequence of deconstructing the male/female dichotomy (Kim, 2003). Thus, characteristics of the "flower boy" are able to satisfy both feminine and masculine qualities.

4

Textual Analysis of *Boys Over Flowers*

The present study used textual analysis to examine the representation of masculinity and male gender roles in the Korean drama *Boys Over Flowers*, available in serial form online at Netflix (http://www.netflix.com/WiMov ie/702 13130?sod =search-autocomplete). An initial viewing of the series allowed for familiarization with the show's characters and general plotlines; this was followed by a closer viewing in which specific aspects of the series were noted, with attention paid to visuals (physical appearance and costuming, settings, and activities), specific dialogue (interactions between the main characters, and main characters with peripheral characters), and overarching storylines. Evaluated here is the composite picture that emerges regarding the portrayals of the four major male characters within the F4 group, because they are the most prevalent male characters, and they are the most important characters that form the male image in the series. The text, in terms of dialogue, imagery, and scenes, is thus assessed using the aforementioned frameworks of: (a) hegemonic Korean masculinity (based on Moon, 2002), (b) millennial masculinity, and (3) the *kkonminam*/"flower boy" characteristics.

The Girls and Boys of *Boys Over Flowers*

Jan Di is a teenager who throughout the series works at multiple jobs to help her working class family to make ends meet. During Episode 1, she goes to deliver laundry to a Shinhwa student, and finds him standing on the rooftop of a building, battered and bloodied, ready to jump. This student had been tormented by the F4 for being a lower status than everyone else. As he attempts to jump, Jan Di reaches out and grabs him, ultimately saving his life. Her own life is changed dramatically when she is offered a scholarship to Shinhwa for her actions. Though the relationship between her and F4 starts out contested, she later becomes close friends with them. A love triangle develops between herself and two of the F4 members, Jun Pyo and Ji Hoo.

Ga Eul is Jan Di's best friend who aspires to become an elementary school teacher. After getting over her relationship with her cheating boyfriend, she soon falls for an F4 member, Yi Jeong, but the feeling is not reciprocated. In the concluding scenes of the series, four years have gone by and Yi Jeong returns to Korea and visits Ga Eul at the elementary school where she teaches. Though not shown onscreen, their becoming a couple is alluded to, hinting at a happily ever after for them. Throughout the series, Ga Eul is shown to be caring, a loyal friend to Jan Di, and a strong believer in notions of romantic love. As the drama progresses, she has a strong influence on the "blossoming" of the object of her affection, as Yi Jeong transforms from a playboy to a more egalitarian man.

The "Flower Boys": The F4

The most prominent male character of *Boys Over Flowers* is the leader of F4, Jun Pyo, who is the heir to the Shinhwa Group, the most successful corporation in South Korea. Jun Pyo's grandfather established the Shinhwa schools so that Jun Pyo had a safe environment in which to grow up and receive a high quality education from the world's leading scholars. Jun Pyo's physical attributes combine macho masculinity with *kkonminam* traits. Oftentimes he is shown shirtless, with a slim body, six-pack abs, and smooth skin. He wears clothing that would be considered in the "Beau Brummel" style: dressing elegantly, and using accessories to showcase that a person may belong to an upper, more luxurious class (Crawford, 2006). Jun Pyo displays this type of fashion by wearing flower-print button down shirts, scarves, peacoats, and tight pants, all in pastel colors. However, counter to his clotheshorse image, Jun Pyo plays rugby, drives race cars, and participates in sword fighting at a martial arts studio. Jun Pyo appears to be high maintenance, pretentious, immature, and stuck-up in the beginning of the series, but as his relationship with female main character Jan Di progresses, his attitude slowly becomes more compassionate and caring.

Ji Hoo is another member of the F4; he is grandson to the former president of South Korea, who became a physician after his term. When he was four years old, Ji Hoo's parents were killed in a car accident he himself instigated when he playfully covered his father's eyes while his father was driving. Physically, Ji Hoo shows strong "flower boy" characteristics: he has long, straight, shiny orange-dyed hair, groomed very well; and often wears vests, sweaters, scarves, and earrings, all in light pastel colors that are nearly transparent at times. Ji Hoo's pastimes and hobbies include both masculine and feminine-typed activities. For example, when he hangs out with his F4 friends, he tends to do what they do, and has a masculine-like competitive mentality while he partakes in those activities. However, when Ji Hoo hangs out with Jan Di, he is oftentimes seen nurturing her, displaying a somewhat feminine-typed persona, such as cooking an elaborate breakfast to cheer her up. At first, Ji Hoo shows compassion because he pitied Jan Di, but he later falls in love with her, creating the love triangle between him, Jan Di, and Jun Pyo. Ji Hoo's personality is portrayed as being sincere and empathetic, qualities that first attracted Jan Di to him, but their relationship ultimately results in a close friendship instead of a romance.

Known as the "Casanova" of F4, Yi Jeong is skilled in all areas of the fine arts, especially pottery, and uses these skills as a tactic for picking up (or "hooking up" with) beautiful girls. His family owns the most prestigious art museum in South Korea. In terms of physical appearance, Yi Jeong wears very dark colors and a lot of tight clothing. His hair is well groomed and straightened quite frequently. He often wears scarves and ascots, along with lavish-looking button-down vests. His body figure is shown to be femininely slim-like, but muscular at the same time, conveying a sense that men are to be fit, but still have muscles to be considered masculine. Yi Jeong has the tendency to participate in masculine activities more so than feminine activities, such as boxing, race car driving, and air riflery. Though quite skilled at feminine-typed activities such as pottery and dancing, Yi Jeong uses these skills to get what he wants from girls, instead of getting to know them. Though he starts off being a "playboy," as the series progresses he slowly transforms to a person who wants to be in a committed relationship with Ga Eul (Jan Di's best friend), and begins to view women less as objects or targets with whom to have romantic flings and more as equals.

Woo Bin is also a playboy, but instead of being a smooth talker, he is known as the "macho man." Woo Bin's family runs a very successful construction company, which also has ties to gang-related activities. In terms of physical appearance, Woo Bin is shown to be the most overtly masculine member of F4, usually wearing dark colors and button-down shirts that reveal parts of his chest. He is often seen hanging out with Yi Jeong more than any of the other F4 members, and the pair regular play sports such as soccer or hockey, or attempting to pick up women at dance clubs. His role in the series is more limited than the other male characters. In terms of personality and behavior, Woo Bin appears tough and fearless. As described by Jan Di in the concluding episode, Woo Bin is the "backbone" of F4 who uses his physical strength to protect all of its members, as well as Jan Di.

The Blossoming of the "New Korean Man"

Character depictions and development as well as story arcs in *Boys Over Flowers* combine to suggest to viewers that the main male characters in the F4 transform from displaying characteristics associated with hegemonic Korean masculinity to exuding a more counterhegemonic masculinity that reflects aspects of the new millennial man and the "flower boy" persona depicted in the *kkonminam* subgenre of the Korean soap opera. Results of this textual analysis of the major storylines of the male characters who get the most airtime and narrative emphasis point to three themes that characterize the "new man" in *Boys Over Flowers*: (a) men as egalitarian, (b) men as expressive best friends to women, and (c) men as protectors of women. With the exception of F4 member Woo Bin, each theme corresponds with a male character's transformation over the course of the series. In a sense, the F4 grow from boys who reflected aspects of hegemonic masculinity into men who reflect a new version of the desired and desirable "Korean man."

The New Korean Man as Egalitarian

The transformation of a traditional version of Korean hegemonic masculinity to a more egalitarian-like male was found in Yi Jeong's storyline, through his progressively growing relationship with Ga Eul. A dismissive attitude toward women that marks the traditional masculinity of Korean culture is illustrated by the F4 in Episode 1, when three of its members, Jun Pyo, Woo Bin, and Yi Jeong, are watching Jan Di getting harassed by other students on a television. While they are watching this, Woo Bin and Yi Jeong make a bet with each other to see how long she could endure the poor treatment. If Woo Bin wins, then Yi Jeong has to give one of his handcrafted bowls to a girl that Woo Bin had been trying to "hook-up" with. If Yi Jeong wins, Woo Bin needs to give him the numbers of girls that he names the "super" girls. This scene shows Yi Jeong's initial feelings about women as being mere prizes.

Another example of Yi Jeong's patriarchal and dismissive attitude toward women occurs in Episode 4. While talking with Ga Eul at his house, Yi Jeong tells Ga Eul that it would be best that Jan Di breaks-up with Jun Pyo, because their relationship is impossible. Ga Eul then leaves Yi Jeong's house angrily. Woo Bin then arrives at Yi Jeong's house and sees Ga Eul angry and asks Yi Jeong if she was mad because Yi Jeong tried to "hit" on her. Yi Jeong smiles and says, "She is not my genre. I really don't like tacky things" (referring to Ga Eul). This scene shows Yi Jeong's tendency to typify girls as objects of sexual desire who exist to please men.

As the series continues, however, Yi Jeong's view of women slowly shifts. After seeing his divorced, professor dad kissing yet another beautiful, younger girl student, he drives off ferociously. While driving around the city, Yi Jeong sees Ga Eul sitting on stairs on the sidewalk in tears, sobbing over the fact that her boyfriend cheated on her. Yi Jeong pulls over, picks her up, and brings her back to his house. He grabs one of his hand-crafted cups and drops it, but it doesn't break. He tells her, "To become strong this is what you have to go through, just like what you went through today" (Episode 9). This scene shows that Yi Jeong is starting to see women as more than objects, and, indeed, shows his capacity for empathy and nurturance. In Episode 18, a flashback memory reveals Yi Jeong's previous attitudes toward women. In the flashback, he remembers a past relationship with a girl; "A girl is like a math problem. I figure it out if I study it a bit more," he tells her. This flashback characterizes that Yi Jeong used to think that women are just objects or problems waiting to be solved.

The denouement of Yi Jeong's journey toward the new man persona occurs in Episode 23, when Ga Eul goes to visit Yi Jeong at his house. Yi Jeong is stepping on clay, when he apologizes to her for his actions when they went to meet his father. Then he asks Ga Eul if she wants to try and step on the clay with him, and she does. This simple image encapsulates Yi Jeong's main storyline: he no longer believes in women as objects, but as equals to men as they step on the clay together, symbolizing his new egalitarian beliefs.

Men as Best Friends to Women

Another part of Korean hegemonic masculinity is a strong belief in traditional Confucian teachings regarding gender inequality and the inappropriateness of male-female friendships. This idea is debunked through Ji Hoo's narrative, as he becomes transformed from a person who holds strong friendships with his fellow male members of F4 exclusively to a person who has a close friendship with a female. His platonic friendship with Jan Di shows that men can have close relationships with women. In Episode 1, when Jan Di is the victim of a mean prank by a group of students and covered in eggs and flour, she runs to a stairway to scream and cry. As she screams at the top of her lungs, Ji Hoo comes out and tells her that she needs to be quiet because she woke him up from his nap. Noticing Jan Di is in distress, he wipes off the mess with his handkerchief. This scene introduces the viewer to Ji Hoo's calm and passionate personality. In Episode 2, as Jan Di comes out of Shinhwa High School's swimming pool, a group of men were about to harm her when Ji Hoo walks in, telling them to stop. As Jan Di thanks Ji Hoo, he tells her, "I wasn't helping you; this kind of stuff just annoys me." Though he rescues her from harm, he still does not respect her, but just helps her out of pity.

Ji Hoo and Jan Di's relationship grows closer as the series progresses. In Episode 9, Jan Di was avoiding Jun Pyo because she felt uncomfortable that they were completely different from each other in terms of financial status and interests. Ji Hoo runs into Jan Di after she had finished swimming, and asked her if he could give her some advice about Jun Pyo. Ji Hoo then tells her not to avoid him, but to give him a chance: "There is no such thing as Jun Pyo's world or Jan Di's world. Just like you and I are from the same world. If it is a burden, you can drag him to yours." Ji Hoo and Jan Di are now at the point that they are comfortable with each other so that they can offer each other advice, to the point that Ji Hoo sees them as coming from the "same world," which shows how Ji Hoo realizes that a girl can be a best friend. An additional example of Ji Hoo's view appears in Episode 13, when he notices that Jan Di was struggling when she was swimming. After visiting a doctor and learning she will never be able to swim competitively again, they go back to the pool, where Jan Di breaks down in tears and says, "I don't know what I'm supposed to do now." Though she is depressed and lost, Ji Hoo embraces her and tells her, "I'll help you. I'll help you. Let's find it together!" Ji Hoo's close friendship with Jan Di is solidified in the final episode, when the series fast-forwards to four years into the future. Jan Di and Ji Hoo both go to the same medical school where they are trying to become doctors. Ji Hoo's journey to "new manhood" involves letting go of strong patriarchal Confucian ideals to embracing the notion that men can be best friends with women and vice-versa.

Violence Repurposed

A third component of Korean hegemonic masculinity is overt militarization. Moon (2002) asserted that through the mandatory two-year service in the South Korean military for men, Korean men are exposed to and are socialized to be overtly violent. This notion of violence as a form of masculinity becomes redirected in *Boys Over Flowers* in terms of the reasons for using violence rather than its requirement as an inherent aspect of masculinity. Here, this aspect of masculinity is reformed from men using violence to get what they want and to show off their might to using violence to protect women's rights. Rather than part of the masculine identity within a patriarchy that maintains gender inequality and the lower status of women, violence as used by the new Korean man becomes symbolic of the need for men to help women, and—taken to its logical conclusion—become participants in the transformation of a traditionally male-dominated society to one that promotes egalitarianism.

This transformation is seen through the narrative of F4 member Jun Pyo. Since Jun Pyo is the main male character throughout the whole series, this may be the most pertinent of all major themes observed. The first form of violence that the viewers are introduced to is the very first scene in Episode 1: Jun Pyo is the aggressor who has been chasing and bullying the male student whom Jan Di eventually rescues from jumping off of a building. The first incident of aggression and violence that Jun Pyo exerts on Jan Di herself is in the last scenes of Episode 1. As Jan Di and her new friend are hanging out and eating ice cream outside, the F4 walk by and Jan Di's friend accidentally spills her ice cream on Jun Pyo's shoe. Even though she apologizes, Jun Pyo tells her to lick the ice cream off of his shoes. Jan Di then stands up for her friend, but Jun Pyo just tells her that if she really was her friend then she should lick off the ice cream for her. Instead, Jan Di grabs her ice cream and shoves it in Jun Pyo's face. Ironically, the rivalry between the aggressive bully Jun Pyo and strong-willed Jan Di—who refuses to accept poor treatment from Jun Pyo—results in Jun Pyo's less violent yet continued and immature ill-treatment of her. As the series progresses, their relationship turns from a rivalry to a romance.

Jun Pyo himself reforms from a man who uses violence to display his power to a man who uses violence to protect Jan Di. For example, Jan Di and Jun Pyo go ice skating on a double date with Ga Eul and her older boyfriend. Ga Eul's boyfriend and Jun Pyo go to get coffee, when Ga Eul's boyfriend gets a phone call. He then tells Jun Pyo that he was going to the club later that night, and that they should go to the club together to get "better" girls. Ga Eul's boyfriend then indirectly insults Jan Di by telling Jun Pyo that he could do better than her. Jun Pyo then beats him up. Though Jun Pyo still uses violence, he uses it to essentially teach the cheating boyfriend—and, by default, the viewer—a lesson about the consequences of treating women badly.

In Episode 12, Jun Pyo's evolution from selfish bully to selfless rescuer becomes complete. A gang of men kidnapped Jan Di, and it is Jun Pyo who goes to the abandoned warehouse where Jan Di is being held. The kidnappers ambush him, and tell him that the only way that he will walk out of the warehouse alive is if he says that he would give up on Jan Di and his relationship with her. Jun Pyo refuses. Then one of the men grabs a chair and as he is about to break it over Jun Pyo, Jan Di jumps over him and the chair breaks over her instead. Jun Pyo does not attempt to save Jan Di for his own self interests, but takes physical abuse from the men so that Jan Di doesn't have to. Though Jun Pyo and Jan Di both end up getting brutally hurt, and the chair ultimately breaks on Jan Di's back, it was Jun Pyo's initial decision to risk his life and use violence to save another.

Conclusion: *Boys Over Flowers* and the Making of the "New Man"

This paper examined hegemonic masculinity and counterhegemonic masculinity as depicted in the K-drama *Boys Over Flowers*. The transformation stories of three of its main male characters provide a composite of the "flower boy" version of the new man, a persona achieved by these males' interactions with the two principal female characters. The self-centered F4 members evolve into young men who come to view women as equals rather than objects, suggesting that men have the capacity to be more egalitarian within a culture that has experienced compressed industrialization; learn how to be trustworthy and expressive best friends with females, debunking the hegemonic ideal that men are to be dominant, while women are to be submissive; and use violence not to exert status but to protect others.

Although *Boys Over Flowers* provides evidence that the "new man" image may be taking hold in Korean mass media, especially texts that target a younger audience, the issue of violence remains part of a man's identity. Though Jun Pyo uses violence to protect others, he still uses violence rather than other means. Additionally, the character of Woo Bin poses a complication to the image of the *totally* new man, in that although his presence remains constant as a member of the F4, the series doesn't give this character much screen time and he doesn't even make an appearance in some episodes. However, his role as the group's "muscle" can be read as keeping this element of masculinity as part of the "flower boy" image: he looks good, cares about his appearance, can be "just friends" with girls, but can still pack a punch.

The findings from this textual analysis are similar to recent literature on the transformation of masculinity as portrayed in Western media. Examples include Gillam and Wooden's (2008) examination of the new man who demonstrates feminine-typed traits in Disney Pixar movies, and blogger Asher-Perrin's (2013) observations regarding the transformation of Dean Winchester in the CW's *Supernatural* from "macho man" to a more sensitive, vulnerable and multifaceted character. These portrayals of the progression of masculinity provide a new definition of what it means to be a "man" in the 21st century, at least in certain media.

Boys Over Flowers offers a culturally based text that illustrates transformation of young men who initially display attitudes that reflect the "old way" of performing the male role in Korean society to ones who appear to be able to develop egalitarian views. Even though a new, more "feminine" masculinity presents a redefined character type in the K-drama, an accompanying "new woman" persona that similarly redefines femininity would enhance the potential for this media form to offer viewers a picture of what gender equity might look like. This in itself indicates the need for future inquiry into the pervasiveness of gender difference as reflected in mass media texts regarding love, romance, and gender roles across cultures and popular media texts.

References

Aldrich, R. (2004). Homosexuality and the city: An historical overview. *Urban Studies, 41*, 1719-1737.

AGB Nielsen Media Research (n.d.). AGB daily ratings. Korea. Retrieved from http://www.agbnielsen.co.kr/index.asp?ref=0.

Asher-Perrin, E. (2013, May 17). *Supernatural's* Dean Winchester dismantled his own maschismo—and that's why we love him [Blog post]. Retrieved from http://www.tor.com/blogs/2013/05/supernaturals-dean-winchester-dismantled -his-own-machismo-and-thats-why-we-love-him.

Beyon, J. (2002). *Masculinities and culture*. Buckingham, UK: Open University Press.

Boys over flowers [n.d.]. *The Korean Movie and Drama Database*. Retrieved from http://www.hancinema.net/korean_drama_Boys_over_Flowers.php

Cho, U. (2013). Gender inequality and patriarchal order recontextualized. In H-Y. Cho, L. Surendra, and H-J. Cho (Eds.), *Contemporary South Korea society: A critical perspective* (pp. 18-27). New York, NY: Routledge.

Crawford, Z. (2006, Spring). Man of the cloth: To Beau Brummell, clothes were a religion. *New York Times Magazine*, 92-93.

DramaFever (2013, July 3). *Boys Over Flowers* American remake to air in late 2013. [Blog post]. Retrieved from http://www.dramafever.com/news/boys-over-flowers-american-remake-to-air-in-late-2013/

Frederick, II, N. (2006). *A couple of white guys sitting 'around talking': Representations of masculinity and commodification in* Frasier. Paper presented at the International Communication Association, Dresden, Germany.

Garde, J. (2003). Masculinity and madness. *Counselling and Psychotherapy Research, 3*(1), 6-16.

Geum, J. (2000). *Korea's seonbi and the seonbi ideology*. Seoul, South Korea: Seoul National University Press.

Gillam, K., & Wooden, S. R. (2008). Post-princess models of gender: The new man in Disney/Pixar. *Journal of Popular Film and Television, 36*(1), 2-8.

Gramsci, A. (1971). *Selections from the prison notebooks* (Q. Hoare & G. Nowell Smith, Trans.). New York, NY: International Press.

Jung, S. (2010). Chogukjeok pan-East Asian soft masculinity: Reading boys over flowers, coffee prince and shinhwa fan fiction. In D. Black, S. Epstein, & A. Tokita (Eds.), *Complicated currents: Media flows, soft power and East Asia* (pp. 1-8). Melbourne, Australia: Monash University ePress.

Kim, Y. (2003). *Cheongae-ui geoul [A thousand mirrors]*. Seoul, South Korea: Saenggag-ui Namu.

Kim, Y., & Han, S. (2006). Homosexuality in ancient and modern Korea. *Culture, Health, and Sexuality, 8*(1), 59-65.

Maliangkay, R. (2010). The effeminacy of male beauty in Korea. *IIAS Newsletter, 55*, 6-7.

Moon, S. (2002). The production and subversion of hegemonic masculinity: Reconfiguring gender hierarchy in contemporary South Korea. In L. Kendall (Ed.), *Under construction*. Honolulu, HI: University of Hawaii Press.

Pompper, D. (2010). Masculinities, the metrosexual, and media images: Across dimensions of age and ethnicity. *Sex Roles, 63*, 682-696.

Sosnoski, D. (1996). *Introduction to Japanese culture*. North Clarendon, VT: Tuttle Publishing.

Blurring the Lines between Biography and Fiction: Writing About Ghosts

Lorna Gibb[A]

I n this article, I consider reflectively how the process of embarking on writing a book within one genre, that of general, popular non-fiction, led to the creation of a novel that hoped to say something about the nature of biography. The topic itself, that of the historically famous and enduring spirit entities, John and Katie King, while rich in historical account and primary source material, lacked chronological cohesion. The novel form allowed this to be constructed while also enabling a consideration of why these non-existent figures achieved the fame that they did, in essence by making them real and believable within the context of the work itself. The use of traditional biographical source material, some real, some fictitious, was used to give credence and support to the story while allowing a thematic exploration of what draws us to some personalities both in life and in literature.

I had been working as a non-fiction writer for a few years, written a couple of well received biographies and a short memoir, and my original thought was to write a non-fiction book about spiritualism. It wasn't a topic that had interested me greatly in the past but while casually researching a vague idea I had about writing a book on the lives of women mediums, I noticed an interesting and somewhat curious phenomenon.

In accounts of many of the séances, in the US, in the UK, in Italy, the Netherlands, even Russia, over a period spanning two centuries, two popular ghosts seemed to be mentioned more than any other. The ghosts of John and Katie King were regularly appearing figures at séances from the mid nineteenth century. They were often the friendly, entertaining face of the séance and as such would be introduced by many mediums in order to draw crowds, either to reinvigorate a failing career or to boost an early one.

Their fame outlasted each of the mediums that presented them and their carefully constructed personae were altered and depicted in accordance with the needs of particular cultures, situations and audiences. A group of learned men in 19th -century Russia in need of guidance on political matters would converse through a medium with an educated and able John King; a group of middle-aged women attending a séance in East London would leave laughing and a little in love with his charming wit. Katie appeared both as

[A] Middlesex University

a matronly woman imparting advice to the lovelorn, and as a scantily clad beauty who would settle on a séance sitter's knee, perhaps stroking him, all in return for a small gift of jewellery.

Both personalities had sprung from a single and unlikely source, a remote farmhouse in Millfield Ohio in the year 1854. However, a book that listed the various accounts would lack narrative cohesion, and so I decided instead to embark upon a novel that would allow me to trace the evolution of the spirit, through the imaginations of its various creators, as well as to consider, while doing so, the nature of biography. When we write about someone's life, we construct a tale using archival evidence and interview. This is the substance of what remains to us. Yet for John and Katie King, who had clearly never existed in any real sense, a similar documentary trail was in evidence.

I wanted to embed this contradiction in a novel while looking at what is known and not known. Thus, most of the details about séances, mediums, and the events that occurred are factual, with one essential difference. My narrator is a ghost who believes in a power greater than itself. It is a novel of parts: letters, documentation, some genuine, some not, sections of old books, as well as new factual accounts woven into the lives of fictitious characters. I was interested in how the myth developed and perpetuated, by what means it spread, and ultimately achieved public consciousness of the kind it had. The myth itself continues to persist even today, although without the widespread international fame of its heyday. This, too, is remarkable.

The Koons were a large farming family in Millfield Towship, Athens County. After the death of his daughter, Filenia, Jonathan Koons rejected his local church, in particular its hellfire and brimstone approach to the afterlife, and instead, tried to convert his neighbors to spiritualism. He did this by organizing séances with his talented family of ten children. The whole family created events using standard tricks such as ventriloquism and sleight of hand, and sensory confusion, all of which were presented in darkness by a voice calling itself John King. Female singing by an accompanying, although as yet unnamed spirit, left audiences eulogising the beauty of an ethereal voice. Both John and the female spirit promised an afterlife of joy and plenty, in marked contrast to the sermons of the local Presbyterian Church.

The meetings were held in a specially built log cabin and through word of mouth, became so successful that travellers from states across most of the country came to participate in them.

The figure of John King achieved an almost folkloric status – he became a local ghostly personality, often sighted at events but also reported as a more traditional ghost haunting crumbling buildings and graveyards (in the graveyard where Filenia is buried there is still much local belief that it is haunted by a spirit 'called up by the old Koons family').

It also led to a battle with the local church. In retaliation Koons published a book about his new found faith.[1] The Koons made many converts; the trickery they used was often believed simply because their motivations were not financial (they never took money for séances and indeed almost bankrupted themselves putting up visitors) but rather spiritual. Jonathan genuinely felt that the established church was a bad thing and wanted people to remain Christians, in the sense of following Christ and believing in God, but to move away from what he saw as a negative and damning interpretation, to one that offered hope and was more in keeping with his kinder ideology. While the techniques of trickery employed undoubtedly involved practice deceit, he thought them a good way of converting people to something he believed to be true, a means that justified the end. The journalist, Charles Partridge was one witness to the Ohio displays and returned to New York to write an article that brought a widespread fame, not so much for the Koons, but to their spirit compere.

One family who thus learned of the Koons gatherings was the Davenports in Buffalo, NY. Ira Senior was a local chief of police, and his two sons were keen entertainers who often amused friends and family gatherings with their skill as magicians and ventriloquists. The two boys persuaded their parents that they were being guided by John King, even going so far as to be reported missing for two days, and claiming afterwards that the ghost had transported them as part of their attempt.

They became what was, at that time, a standard séance act, a mix of trickery and exploitation of people's fascination with the hereafter. Their originality was in the character of the spirit compere who addressed and amused their audiences. John King, the Davenport's spirit guide was sage and funny, a likeable rogue but also a man who could discuss matters of import with men of learning and position. The success of their act and their wish to avoid conscription in 1864 resulted in a European tour. The King character's US fame was quickly matched by a rapturous European reception and the Davenports were invited to the Winter Palace so that the Tsar Nicholas II could ask advice, not from the brothers, but from their 'spirit guide.'

In London his appearance drew huge crowds of the curious and the believing, eager to see the 'American ghost.' When the Davenports returned to the US, John King remained at various locations in Europe, most noticeably in London where he had once again evolved, first into an elderly English ghost at the hands of the mediums Herne and Williams, and then, more surprisingly, into a woman, as female mediumship took center stage.

---

[1] Koons, Jonathan (1853) *A Book for Skeptics: Being Communications from Angels*, State Library of Ohio Rare Books Collection

With Katie King's fame came a whole new order of success, one that involved renowned scientists testing her mediums for trickery, and publicly stating that yes, ghosts existed, and Katie King was one such spirit. Sir William Crookes, the chemist, renowned for his discovery of the element Thalium, believed that Katie was a real entity who regularly materialised for a young London woman, former schoolteacher, Florence Cook.[2] His experiments were meticulous, using photography and electricity, two relatively new discoveries, but failed to expose even the most obvious kind of conjuring trick. As Katie King's UK fame grew, an American rival appeared, with press on both sides of the Atlantic vying to claim that their Katie was the 'real spirit,' was more beautiful, more bewitching. Just as Crookes was convinced by Florence Cook, so the US Katie, the creation of an ex- carnie singer called Eliza White, was busy seducing a former senator of Indiana, the well-known philanthropist, Robert Dale Owen. Like Crookes, Owen had no doubt that Katie was real, to the extent that he fell in love with her, spending every night at séances, showering the slim figure dressed in white who walked among the expectant audiences with gifts of fruit, jewellery and flowers. He wrote of his belief in a piece for the *Atlantic Monthly*, an article which sadly appeared only one day after the fraud perpetuated by White and her accomplices came to light.

Broken both by the loss of a figure that he had come to love, as well as by his ruined reputation, Dale Owen was subsequently admitted to the Indiana Asylum for the Insane.

An imaginary figure had destroyed the lives of two successful and well-loved men.

The King's success continued into the twentieth century. The scandal of the Katie King exposures meant that John King once again gained popularity, in particular at the séances of an Italian medium called Eusapia Palladino. Promoter and ex-medium, the shady Giovanni Damiani transformed Eursapia, a poor girl of the Neapolitan slums, into a spiritual superstar. She was examined at Cambridge University, in New York and by Marie Curie who declared her manifestations to be genuinely spiritual.

However, with the advent of the Great War, the world of spiritualism changed, witty 'compere ghosts' and guides were no longer fashionable as nations grieved the loss of their sons and looked for a message from beyond of how they had passed. Mentions of séances involving John King are scant during this period, and even then, he appears briefly to introduce the spirit of a dead boy, or prepare a gathered group for news from the beyond.

---

[2] See Hall, Trevor (1985) *The Medium and the Scientist*, Prometheus Books, for an account of this relationship, although not all relevant contemporary documentation is used or cited therein.

For a few decades, after the 1930s, there was no mention of either King ghost at all; it was as if the fame has dissipated, gradually dwindling with the fashions of the eras. But then in 1974, a successful Italian television medium called Fulvio Rendhell announced that Katie King would appear at his séance, and a young, Victorian clad woman, claiming to be the spirit Katie, was witnessed by a huge audience in Rome.

This heralded a new dawn of interest in the once-renowned spirits. In Cesenatico, a small Adriatic town between Rimini and Ravenna, a bookshop, specialising in spiritualism and the occult, is named after her; she is still sighted in various locations around Europe.

When I was writing the novel, I decided it was about time Katie was introduced to the digital age, so I gave her a twitter account, @ghostlykatie, tweeted a couple of times about non corporeality, and fake mediumship (the ghost in my novel scorns fakery) and waited. In a short time she had over a thousand followers.

Perpetuating a myth it seems was made even easier by the web. Yet, I thought, it was a far cry from what she had once been, and I allowed my protagonist to lament, "I am a ghost in the machine when I have been a spirit that haunts humanity."

What I had originally thought would be a non-fiction book was now a novel that was also a book about biography and a treatise on the nature of faith, of belief. Recently Professor Richard Wiseman has written papers carefully describing the manner of trickery and prestidigitation used by Palladino. Yet, I mused, while reading online comments and counter arguments on his scholarly work, it had no impact on those who were convinced of the reality of a spirit world.

'The use of trickery, and its discovery, shows only that, not more. Because some people create me, imagine me, impersonate me and use trickery to do so, does not mean I do not exist and proves nothing, nothing at all.'

Katie and John's longevity, an odd term to describe something that never lived, never existed at all, had outlasted those who would deny them.

---

[3] Wiseman, Richard (1993) 'Barrington and Palladino: Ten major errors' *Journal of the Society for Psychical Research 59* (830) 16-34.

Singing the Same Song: The Unsettling Celebration of Homogenous Artistry Encouraged by *American Idol*

Josh Bates[A] & Kristin M. Barton[A]

Music is an invaluable outlet of expressiveness and creativity that thrives on originality. But recently the quality of music produced in contemporary society has taken a backseat to record sales. What was once appreciated for not only its profitability, but also its vitality and resonance with listeners has eroded into a uniform, money-generating colossus. A guiding wind in veering the musical vessel off course is *American Idol* (2001–present), navigating the sonic waters by promoting talent in the form of an individual's ability to replicate other artists' tones and pitches, not his or her creative capacity or musical eccentricity. Granted, the program's viewership has hit record lows, with a 33% viewership drop from seasons 11 to 12 (Keveney), but its negative impact on musical communities cannot be ignored. The television series has excused a lack of rhythmic and melodic originality by elevating chiming clones instead of authentic artists, and the result is a widespread prelation for a genre of generic music. Artists such as Katy Perry, Carly Rae Jespen (who placed third on season three of Canadian Idol), and Nickelback dominate the charts, despite the fact that artists such as these who are not widely known for their musical prowess (Tongson). As a result, America's palate for creatively inspiring music has been numbed by the homogenous flavors now offered on the radio.

The Singing Competition

American Idol was born from the British series *Pop Idol*, a reality-singing competition that aired from 2001–2003. Based on its UK predecessor, *American Idol* began airing on Fox in June, 2001, at which time it became an instant success, garnering 9.9 million viewers on its first night (Rushfield). In order to eliminate participants, the show not only enlists a panel of judges that critique performances, but also solicits votes from viewers. The show's commercial success was staggering. Millions of voters demonstrated each week their level of emotional investment in the performers. For example, viewers and fans of the *Idol* star Kelly Clarkson elevated her recording of "A Moment Like This" to the # 1 spot within a week, rivaling the chart movement of the Beatles' 1964 hit "Can't Buy Me Love." Now a franchise, the show has

---

[A] Dalton State College

hit such disparate places as Poland and South Africa, and has been copied by regional networks and local stations (Stahl). The intention of connecting the show to the homogenous state of the music industry is not to attack *Idol*'s entertainment value or demerit its popularity; instead the aim is to illuminate the correlation between this talent-based reality show and the erosion of diverse and interesting output from the music industry.

Erosion of Musical Variety

Research shows little evidence to promote any assertion of *Idol*'s direct relationship with the homogenous state of the music industry, but the industry's declining quality is almost without contention. Serrà, Boguná, Haro, and Arcos, researchers at the Artificial Intelligence Research Institute of the Spanish National Research Council in Barcelona, examined the changes in sonic characteristics of music through a quantitative analysis of almost half a million songs and found that a homogenization has occurred over time, one in which artist variety and disparity has become less enterprising. The research team focused on three aspects in the songs: 1) timbre (which refers to the sound texture or color; e.g. the same note would sound different when played on a violin than a human voice singing); 2) pitch (the ordering of tonality in a scaled-frequency; i.e. the distinction between chords, melodies, and tonal arrangements); and 3) loudness (the intrinsic values proprietary to a recording, not the listener's control of audible levels). Serrà et al. compiled data that illustrate the overall diminution of music's "timbral palette" and "pitch content," and the steady increase of its overall loudness, which gives little salute to dynamic diversity. Simply put, songs have become more uniform and less sonically adventurous.

It could be argued that many artists today are pushing the sonic envelope with the amazing technological advancements now available for musical creation. Indeed, technology has afforded musicians ample means of creating new sounds and even new genres (dubstep, vaporwave, future garage), but the argument here is not one of opportunity, or even of advancement; it is one of analogous saturation. The pervasion of these opportune means has uprooted a diverse garden of music and planted systematically manicured singles in its stead.

Defining Original Music

Humans have a profound connection with music. Infants gravitate towards pleasing sounds and turn from discordant ones (Weinberger); parents sing their children to sleep; church congregations unite in vocal accord; fans gather together in song at concerts; music can even trigger nostalgia and soothe tension. Although neuroscientists do not yet have complete and ultimately satisfying answers for the mystery of the universal bond between humans and music, research has provided ample proof of the neurological and psychological effects of the brain's interaction with music. Music engages not just one region of the brain, but almost every neural system and subsystem; the areas of activation can differ based upon the individual's personal experiences and musical aptitude or instruction. During a series of profound operations, the mind processes music through functional segregation (Levitin), placing distinct musical elements across a neurological map in order to analyze and dissect the signals as they come together to form the representation that results in our comprehension of what has been heard. The varying degrees of listening to music – such as simply hearing a song, tapping one's foot along with the radio, singing with friends, or playing an instrument – all create complicated reactions that interact with a variety of brain structures, including the subcortical structures (cochlear nuclei, the brain stem, the cerebellum), the auditory cortices, the hippocampus, the frontal lobe, and the Broca's and Wernicke's areas. Moving further into the mystery of experiential listening, the primitive structures of the cerebellar vermis and the amygdala are involved in the emotions that are felt when processing music (Levitin).

Defining Unoriginal Music

Simon Frith says that labeling music as "bad" or "good" is rather pointless, unless for the sake of an argument, since preferences that result in these adjectives are mostly subjective. This is not to say that arguments are simply a matter of taste, but without knowing an individual's musical inclinations or how she makes sense of her listening pleasures, it can be rather difficult to persuade her to change her opinion about the quality of her preferred music. Studies show that musical preferences are largely "sown in the womb" (Levitin 227), and an extended period of acculturation after birth allows time for an infant to absorb the musical culture in which she is born into. Of course, the human brain is constantly developing throughout infancy, so it can be expected that the evolution of an individual's musical tastes will be no different. Just as with any other personal preference, we are also largely influenced by the opinions of others; but particularly with music, there are certain boundaries, or limitations, that ae internally set with regard to our musical gauges. Levitin says that, "People may tell you that Schonberg is brilliant, or that Tricky is the next Prince, but if you can't figure out what is going on in the first minute or so of one of their pieces, you may find yourself wondering if the payoff will justify the effort you spend trying to sort it all out" (237). Therefore the argument for or against certain types of music is not about persuasion as much as it is about defining ways to discern quality or originality.

Understanding that musical inclinations are subjective unfortunately does not allow the dismissal of music that is clearly lacking in certain departments that require effort and talent in order to sustain enjoyable content, e.g. correct pitch, melodic continuity, and rhythmic organization. Frith notes that there are three types of tracks that feature such a disregard for these necessary components: 1) Tracks which are clearly incompetent musically 2) Tracks organized around "misplaced sentiments or emotions" (18) and 3) Tracks involving genre confusion. To say that *American Idol* is responsible for some of the "bad" music thriving today is not to relate the series to the first type of track discussed by Frith, meaning most artists seen on the show contribute songs to the music communities that are musically competent. But many awkwardly sentimental songs, as well as multi-genre songs, have been released by artists who have found success through the talent-based show.

For example, Clay Aiken, who on May 21, 2003, was runner-up at the end of *Idol*'s second season and went on to be that season's highest selling artist (Barnes), represents Frith's second and third distinctions. In his 2006 release, "A Thousand Days," Aiken sings, "...if I gave you the moon, would you notice that I'm right beside you?" and "You're the sun that shines and lights up the evening skies." While certainly a sentimental simile, Aiken's iterations are not necessarily unique (Thanki). His use of familiar literary devices does not negate his vocal talent, nor does it imply that the larger body of his lyrical content is as equally conventional; but it does exemplify the argument that links *Idol* to the homogeneity of music today and Frith's argument against "misplaced sentiments."

American Idol

Forman states that, for musicians, an appearance on television was not simply an outlet for musical expression; it was a pathway to greater success in the entertainment industry. This is to say that, although talent is displayed during the competition, many viewers do not watch the show just to increase their musical aptitude or to discover fresh and creative musicianship. Stahl implies that many viewers tune in because they resonate with the contestant's dreams of success, and they want to provide their voting support. Stahl suggests, as does Gamson, that true stardom (fame that is legitimately earned) involves a "complex and paradoxical relationship with the target audience: aspiring idols must demonstrate both specialness and ordinariness, distance and closeness, similarity and difference, particularly regarding social position" (217). Stahl further concedes that *Idol's* narratives promote this authentic humility among the contestants, helping to cultivate the relationships between fans and their idols. Not only does the show fulfill an emotional or resonant need with viewers, but as Barton recognizes, we "watch them sing and dance" because our entertainment needs are gratified. Many fans find the mistake-ridden auditions to be the most captivating element of the show; the embarrassing attempts of contestants are a renewable source of humor on the Internet.

Understanding and admitting these reasons for viewership does not allow the dismissal of the implications of watching and supporting the show's musical content. The show has set a new definition for musical talent, and it not based on creativity or originality. As Simon Cowell (2003), the *Idol* judge known for his coarse honesty, admits, judges and producers do not intend to find the next prolific songwriter or the next pianist who offers a new way to sing counterpart melodies over her chord progressions. The harsh judge concedes that it is his duty, a shared responsibility with the rest of the industry, to "find out who is really marketable and why. The rest is wasted time and wasted breath" (2). After granting that it his job to sell records, Cowell elaborates that he must separate the "wannabes from the real stars" (3). He goes on to explain the difficulty of finding success as a pop star, or in the music industry period. Not everyone can achieve the lyrical notoriety of Bob Dylan or the piano and vocal talent of Elton John. Therefore, record companies need to find something in an artist that will ultimately help sell records.

American Idol and similar shows are platforms for this success, and judges like Simon Cowell know how to scout the marketable attributes that will turn a contestant into an idol. This argument is not explicitly casting blame upon the judges or the producers of the show; they are all involved in a business after all. But this incidental steering of America's musical preferences as a result of the judges' and producers' intentions is alarming, simply because, as discussed previously, the relationship between humans and music is invaluable. Fortunately, Cowell is quick to add that the foundation to an artist's successful career is that the artist has some degree of real musical talent, so he is not advocating that the industry create stars out some sort of musical void. But despite his reassuring clarification, it is clear that *Idol* has permitted a marketable and unvarying formula to dictate what musical talent is, and America has adopted the same standards.

These standards have caused viewers to gravitate away from the artistry of well-respected and popular musicians. What if the renowned American singer/songwriter Bob Dylan were to compete for the *Idol* crown? Dylan's voice has so few traces of marketable talent that it is unlikely that the accomplished lyricist would advance beyond the initial audition rounds of the competition. The contrasts between Dylan and the TV series are just too great. As Unterberger distinguishes, Dylan represents the purity of American songwriting, creating his own music and lyrics, and refining his craft with elements of folk, country, and even gospel music. Representing musical creativity and talent, Dylan brings a personal and unique stylistic approach to his music and shares a worldview with his audience, all traits of genuine and refreshing artistry. Practically opposing this variety and musical finesse is *American Idol*, "approach[ing] the history of American music as one big popular songbook, to be regurgitated and occasionally re-interpreted but never added to or advanced, celebrating originality at times but mostly valuing the ability to conform to pre-existing pop ideals" (Unterberger 3). If these assertions are not proof enough of the disparity between the show and diverse musical talent, even Cowell doesn't hesitate to agree. "A singing poet? It just bores me to tears," claimed Cowell. "I've got to tell you, if I had 10 Dylans in the final of 'American Idol,' we would not be getting 30 million viewers a week. I don't believe the Bob Dylans of this world would make 'American Idol' a better show" (3).

Steering the Musical Vessel Off-Course

Although contestants that advance in the competition must possess clear vocal talent, the series has sadly conditioned audiences to expect different attributes from an artist than just commendable vocal skills. Viewers want to see beautiful people contending with each other; they want to share struggles with the contestants that have worked so hard to compete on the show; they want to believe that an everyday person from Texas can become a pop star (Rushfield). Much of the competition's appeal is even unrelated to the performers. The emotionally and visually stunning overtures are derived from the glamorous and elaborate set construction and the musical talent (the performers that enable singers to accompany live music) backing the contestants. According to Rushfield, the crew labored to add to the intensity of the show's format in season three. The wardrobe, makeup, lighting, and set design teams all crafted makeovers for the stage and the contestants; the backdrops became more gallant, the direction segues became more fluid, and the cameras became more adventurous, magnifying the energy and emotion by sweeping across all angles to capture dramatic or quiet moments. For those with behind-the-scenes access to this creative environment, it is understood that its team of professionals are "the best in the world at what they do" (Rushfield 135). When *Idol* contestants have successful careers, Americans relate their success to the themes and aesthetics of the show, reducing the likelihood that viewers will find merit in artists such as Bob Dylan, who as stated before, clearly would fail to advance on the show. A viewer's psychological perspective of musical talent becomes obscured when watching the show (Levitin). There is not much similarity between watching *American Idol* and viewing a songwriting showcase at Nashville's Bluebird Café or attending a rock concert at Atlanta's Variety Playhouse. The former perpetuates a desire to watch the "divas [fall]" or rise (Rushfield 135), while the latter examples promote the originality and creative musicality of the artists.

The *Idol* competition is not without merit in terms of musical talent, but an accomplished artist that advances from round to round can still deliver a wanting number, particularly when he or she merely replicates the tones of the artist whom originally performed the song. Caryn James of the *New York Times* writes, "The music and arrangements [of *American Idol*] are trite, full of wannabe Whitney Houston and Stevie Wonder wails. Originality is a losing strategy." With this in mind, it is arguable that any musical product "conceived, manufactured and marketed" (Stahl 217) around *American Idol* can carry value outside of its use as a commercial asset. "'Idol...is a slick new step in music marketing," laments *Boston Globe* writer Matthew Gilbert, "it's not some kind of altruistic attempt to give a young performer a chance at the big time; it's the first leg in a marketing campaign that will culminate in CD sales. We aren't the TV audience – we're the focus group." This assertion further illuminates that the show has, whether intentional or not, the ability to influence what viewers (the focus group) find appealing when listening to music.

Charting the Progression of Popular Music

Due to the subjectivity of ever-changing musical tastes and preferences, research must include the examination of a myriad of objective songwriting components and musical elements, including (but not limited to): harmonic content; dynamics; mixing (the spatial arrangements of instrumentation); song structure (formatting sections such as verse, chorus, and bridge) and length; and lyrical content. These elements must be defined and appropriated in terms of their relevance for distinguishing between music that is diverse and meaningful and music deemed homogenous and unsubstantial. Analyzed within the context of popular songs both before and after the creation and airing of *American Idol*, these musical components can be used to measure not only the differences between the aforementioned song distinctions, but also to determine a causal relation, if any, between *Idol* and the proposed decline in original and interesting music.

A look at the progression of increased similitude in chart-topping music in the past three decades of *Rolling Stone*'s (hereafter abbreviated *RS*) top-ranked lists reveal a parallel to the unvarying music of today and the advent of *American Idol*. In June, 1981, the top five albums (singles were not ranked at this time), as charted by RS, were from the following artists: 1) REO Speedwagon 2) Steve Winwood 3) The Who 4) STYX 5) Rush (*RS*, 1981). This top five includes "alternative-rock bands," "arena-rock bands," and an R&B soul-singer. By June, 1990, the magazine expanded the top-ranked lists to incorporate the expansion of growing musical artistry. The top 5 singles at this time were from: 1) Sinead O'Connor 2) Madonna 3) Heart 4) Janet Jackson 5) Michael Bolton. Found in this category are solo female artists with disparate qualities, a female rock band, and a soulful male singer/songwriter.

This month also included a top "Dance Tracks" list, featuring 1) Depeche Mode 2) Nine Inch Nails 3) Hi Tek 3 4) Nitzer Ebb 5) Beloved. Not only did *RS* add an entirely separate list to represent the variety of popular artistry, the list itself includes an array of diverse artists. June, 1991, shows the top 5 singles from the artists 1) Roxette 2) Rod Stewart 3) Mariah Carey 4) Amy Grant 5) Cathy Dennis. The top dance tracks are from 1) EMF 2) Latour 3) C&C Music Factory 4) Jesus Jones 5) XYMOX. Again, the top singles remain spread across a variety of styles and artistry. By comparing only the top three songs (succinct research best serves the format of this particular study) from a variety of years, the growing trend of homogenous output from the music industry can be identified objectively. The purpose here is to demonstrate the diversity and creativity involved in song-making; a melody played on guitar may not sound as innovative as the same melody being played on an accordion or a banjo, and when radio is saturated with certain sounds, creative artists and producers seek to incorporate original sounds. Therefore, these artists and producers may elect to use a variety of instrumentation to increase the harmonic content and the energy, or use sparse instrumentation to decrease the content and give a song subtle expression. The same methods can be used in mixing and structuring a song. Making the instruments louder than the vocals (mixing) or beginning a song with a bridge or a chorus instead of a verse (structure) can be ways to express creativity when recording a song (all charts used in this study are from June issues and available from www.rollingstone.com).

Table 1

Top Singles and Dance Singles (June 1991)

		Artist	Song
Singles	1	Roxette	"Joyride"
	2	Rod Stewart	"Rhythm of My Heart"
	3	Mariah Carey	"I Don't Wanna Cry"
Dance	1	EMF	"Unbelievable"
	2	Latour	"People Are Still Having Sex"
	3	C&C Music Factory	"Here We Go"

The songs from the 1991 *RS* rankings, while sharing many commonalities distinctive to the time period (e.g. similar instrumentation, similar mixes and compression elements), also clearly contain a rich variety of musical elements. The list includes energetic pop songs, soulful ballads, and upbeat, electronic dance tracks. Concerning musical talent and originality, Rod Stewart gained popularity for his distinctively raspy vocal tones (Coleman), while Mariah

Carey gained numerous accolades because of her tremendous vocal range and tonality (Caramanica). Both artists brought a refreshing perspective of musicality along with their chart topping success, adding to the diversity of musicianship of the time period. This trend of musical variety and invigorating artistry continued throughout the nineties with artists such as Notorious B.I.G, Naughty by Nature, The Cure, Red Hot Chili Peppers, U2, Sheryl Crow, Dave Mathews Band, Garbage, Busta Rhymes, and Santana. Although they encompass a variety of genres (rock, acoustic rock, rap, grunge, arena rock, funk rock, pop rock), each of these artists added something unique to the canon of music when they emerged and their songs began to climb the charts, ranging from lyrical content, recording methods, unconventional chord progressions, or genre-interfusion. For example, when she released her first album, *Tuesday Night Music Club*, Sheryl Crow was noted for her impressive sense of musicality, merging folk, classic rock, singer/songwriter, and pop rock elements to shape her sound (Buskin).

A gradual decrease in artistic diversity begins to be represented in RS's charts, starting in June, 2001 (corresponding with the first airing of *American Idol*), to 2013. Arguably, this could only be an indication of listeners' changing musical preferences over time, unrelated to the TV series, but the charts do reflect an increasing similitude of artistry, as well an emergence of multi-genre-infused compositions, which operates parallel to the show's success. Below are the musical components of the 2001 rankings.

Table 2

Top Rock and Hip-Hop Singles (June 2001)

		Artist	Song
Rock	1	Staind	"It's Been Awhile"
	2	Weezer	"Hashpipe"
	3	Incubus	"Drive"
Hip-Hop	1	Destiny's Child	"Survivor"
	2	Janet	"All For You"
	3	2Pac	"Until the End of Time"

While this is a very small sample, it is representative of what can be seen on the *RS* charts during this time. These varying musical elements alone are not indicative of influence from *American Idol*, but as the popular music of American culture progresses from 2001 (*Idol*'s first airing) to the present, a gradual decrease in song diversity is audibly noticeable. From 2002 to 2008, the charts are topped by artists such as Nickelback, Puddle of Mudd, Maroon 5, T-Pain, Avril Lavigne, Daughtry (fronted by Chris Daughtry, the fourth place contestant on Idol's fifth season), Fall Out Boy, and Seether. While still containing genre diversity (hard rock, rap, pop rock, alternative rock), the popular songs begin to contain and utilize many of the same elements. The various forms of rock songs begin to use electronically sampled drum loops similar to the popular rap songs. Rap songs incorporate loud and crushing guitar rhythms and sounds. And whether pop, rock, or rap, popular tracks all start to become overly compressed, weakening the dynamic diversity of the top-selling artists. Again, this homogenous interfusion of styles cannot be directly attributed to *American Idol*, but it is notable that before 2001, popular songs were sonically more diverse because of increased harmonic content and smoothly compressed dynamics. However, after *American Idol* began to influence the definition of popular music in American culture, the music industry began to rely heavily on a singular template that encompasses a variety of sounds.

By 2009, *RS* foregoes the distinction between genres in its top-rated lists and simply rates songs via iTunes sales. Again, this in itself is not an indication of Idol's influence over consumer's perception of popular music, but it does reveal parallel activity, which is to say that as the talent-based TV series grew in popularity, so too did a blurring of musical genres and artistic disparity proliferate. Top ranking artist from 2009–2013 include Black Eyed Peas, Katy Perry, Lady Gaga, Maroon 5, Justin Bieber, fun., and Carly Rae Jepsen. The top 5 lists shared by these artists contain fewer divergent songs, making no distinction between genres; instead, all of the songs rest on the laurels of proven sale-tactics in song composition and harmonic content, such as hip hop beat-orientations and electronically augmented vocal effects. The distinct homogenization of popular music is clearly recognizable with the songs charted in *RS*'s 2013 list (top 5 instead of top 3 to allow for possible expansion of diversity).

Table 3

Top Singles (June 2013)

		Artist	Song
Singles	1	Macklemore & Ryan Lewis	"Can't Hold Us"
	2	Pink (feat. Nate Ruess)	"Just Give Me a Reason"
	3	Justin Timberlake	"Mirrors"
	1	Selena Gomez	"Come & Get It"
	2	Imagine Dragons	"Radioactive"

Each of the artists represented above share a mix of rock, pop, and electronic content; whereas popular artists pre-2001 were independently adding variety to the charts, not sharing fashionable music-trends. While a keen listener may be able to distinguish subtle nuances between these songs that could promote genre disparity and arguably provide the artists with faint shades of variety (such as Macklemore's hip hop tonality, Pink's pop sensibility, and Imagine Dragons' rock overtures), all of the artists in *RS*'s June, 2013, top 5 list share similarly catchy hooks (memorable melodies) and pulsing, dance-like rhythms, derived from the electronically generated beats and synthesized chord progressions.

To say that a parallel activity exists between the industry's homogenous musical output beginning in 2001 and *American Idol* is not to imply that there were no homogenous songs before the show; it is to indicate that this lack of disparity has been perpetuated by the talent-based competition and has decreased America's overall desire for creative and fresh music. Music is a compelling medium that is crucial to the lives of listeners (Levitin); it is an artistic expression unlike any other in its ability to combine auditory, visual, and memory-based activity. A song can please the listener as it travels from the ears through the brain's membranes, causing the individual to recall vivid images, and heighten one's mood. The medium is invaluable, and it is important that research is performed to preserve its integrity. Future studies in this area may be able to expose more expansive results of the homogenous musical content of popular music today. By using more scientific calculations of pitch content and decibel levels (similar to the research conducted by Serrà et al.) within contemporary songs, a further decrease in musical diversity may be revealed.

The Call of the Colonial: Jack London's *Martin Eden*

Philip Castille[A]

J ack London's novel *Martin Eden* was not a commercial success when it appeared in 1909, perhaps because it was before its time. Now it stands as his finest and most authentic statement on class and artistic identity. *Martin Eden* maintains a place alongside notable early twentieth-century British and American autobiographical novels of the emerging male artist— among them D. H. Lawrence's *Sons and Lovers*, James Joyce's *A Portrait of the Artist as a Young Man*, Theodore Dreiser's *The 'Genius,'* Sherwood Anderson's *Winesburg, Ohio*, F. Scott Fitzgerald's *This Side of Paradise*, and William Faulkner's *Mosquitoes*. Showing its originality, *Martin Eden* predates all of these Künstlerromane -- novels that draw on biographical detail to portray the young artist. Further, *Martin Eden* is one of first American novels to challenge the Horatio Alger myth, standing alongside turn-of-the-century novels by Dreiser, Stephen Crane, William Dean Howells, and Harold Frederic. These works and others undercut this rags-to-riches story and share a fascination with failure. *Martin Eden* is the first American novel to portray a social-climbing poor white male who rises to commercial "success" only to self-destruct. Indeed, Martin Eden is the template for the modern American male protagonist who vaults upward but falls to pieces; notable instances of this genre are Fitzgerald's *The Great Gatsby* and Norman Mailer's *The American Dream*. After years of self-education and feverish apprentice writing, young Martin Eden soars from the slums to celebrity status as a bestselling author. But he falls victim to a severely split consciousness that puts him at war with himself. In an existential panic Martin abandons art and the city altogether. He answers the call of the colonial by seeking to reinvent himself as an adventurer in the South Seas. But on his voyage to Tahiti he gives up his quest and drops overboard in mid-ocean. This is his weary end, the last in a series of self-defeating choices during his identity crisis.

London's novel is told by an omniscient narrator, who introduces us to a jaunty, unemployed sailor from Oakland who is "almost twenty-one" years old (London, *Martin Eden* 57). On the ferry Martin Eden wins a fistfight to protect an upper-class man, Arthur Morse, from being mugged. For his bravery, Martin is rewarded with a dinner invitation to the Morse mansion in Oakland. Martin does not realize that he is meant to provide the evening's entertainment, telling nautical stories and transporting the idle rich on his "flood of rough eloquence,

---

[A] University of Houston-Victoria

enthusiasm, and power" (52). London treats this opening-scene dinner party as a voyage of discovery; Martin is bedazzled by the "new world" of bourgeois leisure and plenty he encounters in the Morse home. He also is enchanted by Arthur's sister Ruth, a university student who embodies the genteel cultural values of the house she inhabits. After this life-changing evening Martin feels inadequate and becomes dissatisfied with his scruffy North Oakland and Berkeley neighborhoods. He experiences severe dislocation and is never "at home" again in the novel (Reesman 217). He vows to shed his working-class identity, signified by his sunburn and callouses. He will seek to rise intellectually and become worthy of Ruth by becoming a successful author. He burns through his huge resources of vitality and willpower while pounding out stories and compiling a stack of rejected manuscripts.

When acclaim and royalties come after two years of poverty and overwork, they arrive too late. He has become disgusted by the market-driven mechanisms of publication, the fickle tastes of the book-buying public, and the conventional values of his Ruth and her society circle. Martin understands that "It was the bourgeoisie that bought his books and poured gold into his money-sack," but his self-satisfied readers "could not possibly appreciate or comprehend what he had written" (*Martin Eden* 441-2). Martin is dismayed to find himself commodified by publishing machinery that markets him as a proletarian prodigy who rose from deckhand to famous writer. These market forces ignore his intrinsic worth but soar with his "appreciation in value" as a bestselling author (*Martin Eden* 460). He also resents that his own Horatio Alger life story is used to validate the *laissez-faire* myth of American economic and social fluidity. Even though he has two bestsellers at once, Martin is unimpressed by his success. He vows to abandon both art and America for the tropics; "the South Seas were calling to him" and promising a life of imperial adventure in the islands (*Martin Eden*, 420).

Martin answers the call of the colonial in the last winter of his life and sails for Tahiti, which promises that he "will be rejuvenated and revitalized once in the edenic setting of the South Sea Island" (Kim 14). Martin has been to Polynesia before in his former identity as "Mart Eden, the sailor" (*Martin Eden* 453). Now he will return with a newly-constructed identity—not the author, but a swashbuckling Edwardian treasure hunter. He is in search of indigenous resources such as pearls to extract from Pacific waters on the sleek schooner he intends to purchase. He fantasizes that this eroticized vessel will be a lithe, witch-like, female talisman (*Martin Eden* 420)—an implied rejection of the rigid western sexual morality that suppresses female sensuality and constricts male desire. In his gendered ambitions Martin resembles other white adventurers in London's South Sea writings, such as David Sheldon, the slaveholding copra planter in *Adventure* (1911). This was the action novel that Jack London wrote after *Martin Eden*, beginning in 1908. *Adventure* hails "Euro-American racial dominance and entrepreneurial daring in the tropics" (Castille, "*Adventure*," 333) and salvages the colonial dream that perished with Martin Eden in mid-Pacific. Dave seeks to become a South Seas trader and supply commodities for an expanding, globalized market—much as Martin Eden himself has been exploited to supply the bourgeois literary marketplace.

Both *Martin Eden* and *Adventure* are literary products of the cruise of the *Snark*. In 1907, Jack London, his wife Charmian and a small crew had left Oakland on what was intended to be an around-the-world voyage, beginning with a transit of the Pacific Ocean. London was a 31-year-old celebrity author who kept a sharp eye on the literary marketplace. Much as the hard Yukon Northland had defined London's identity and early writing career, now the vast tropical Pacific would serve as the site of his self-dramatization and literary production. Again he would impose his iron will and employ his superb body to master the overwhelming natural forces surrounding him. He would then turn his physical achievements into texts for commercial distribution and monetize his costly voyage on the *Snark*, his custom-built craft. However, because of illness, breakdown and malaise, he abandoned the cruise in December 1908 in the British Solomon Islands, barely a third of the way around the globe.

Jack London, who had promoted himself as a perfect evolutionary specimen, was a very sick man. He was suffering from rotting teeth, malarial fevers, diarrhea, an ulcerated rectum, yaws (a bacterial disease that causes lesions), and another frightening ailment that thickened parts of his skin with silvery white scale (which he feared might be leprosy). London himself had endured racial decline and inferiority in the Melanesian Pacific, where he had succumbed to "the very forces of 'natural selection' ironically and actually represented by his deteriorating white skin" (Phillips 91). He was only 32 years old, and he was humiliated by his physical degeneration in the green hell of Melanesia. Even worse than his ailments was the cure. He treated himself and his crew with a highly toxic mercury-chloride salt, applied to deep, open sores. Giving up the cruise, the Londons took a steamer from Guadalcanal to Sydney. There, Jack had rectal surgery and received arsenic treatments for his mysterious skin disease, diagnosed as severe psoriasis, which causes swathes of skin to peel off. At the hospital he also was given opium for pain relief; this was the start of his drug dependency, which was severe by the time of his death. Also, the mercury and arsenic "medical" treatments he received almost certainly damaged his renal system. Chronic uremia led to kidney and heart failure, bringing on his early death in 1916 at age 40 (Sinclair 157, 246; Reesman 110). Despite his collapse on the *Snark*—and the collapse of his self-concept as an Aryan superman—the voyage was a success for text-production. London gathered material for a great deal of non-fiction, including his bestselling travel book *The Cruise of the Snark* (1911). He also wrote some of his best fiction during and after the voyage, much of it based on his "encounter" experiences with indigenous peoples.

London had toyed for years with a "struggling writer" novel (Watson, "Composition," 402) before he began *Martin Eden* in the summer of 1907 in Honolulu; he continued it while he sailed the *Snark* to French Polynesia. To settle some business affairs in California, he and Charmian took a steamship from Tahiti to San Francisco and back. London worked on *Martin Eden* during this voyage, and he finished it in late February 1908 in Pape'ete, Tahiti, where the *Snark* was docked. London was 32, and the biographical identification that he felt with title character is apparent; Martin Eden's initials spell "ME." The manuscript had several working names, including the ambiguous title "Success." Before publication by Macmillan in1909, London settled on the title *Martin Eden*. While the book was in press, the *Snark* left Tahiti and voyaged westward. London and his crew eventually sailed into Melanesia and the Coral Sea region, where the *Snark* voyage ended in physical and mental breakdown.

Much like his creator, Martin Eden has been to Polynesia (but not yet to Melanesia). Martin recounts his vivid memories of visiting Hawaii as a young sailor—only a few years after Hawaii was annexed by the U.S. in 1898 as part of an expanding American colonial empire. Martin recalls this thrilling encounter with the colonized Pacific:

> He lay on a coral beach where the coconuts grew down to the mellow-sounding surf. The hulk of an ancient wreck burned with blue fires, in the light of which danced the *hula* dancers to the barbaric love-calls of the singers, who chanted to tinkling *ukuleles* and rumbling tom-toms. It was a sensuous, tropic night. In the background a volcano crater was silhouetted against the stars. (*Martin Eden* 55)

With these powerful, sensuous memories as inspiration, Martin writes at least one "Hawaiian story" for the magazines during his literary apprenticeship (Martin Eden 356). He also deepens his knowledge about Hawaii by conversing with his Oakland landlady Maria, a Portuguese woman from the Azores; she migrated to Hawaii to work in the cane fields (*Martin Eden* 260). Martin's most vivid memory of Hawai'i occurs when he jumped ship and stumbled into a leper colony—apparently the same one visited by Jack London on Molokai (London, *Cruise of the* Snark, Chapt VII). Martin tells his fiancée Ruth he was detained there for three months, long enough to become sexually involved with a beautiful Island woman, who was in the first stage of leprosy. Martin fondly recalls this interracial affair and remembers his lover as an earthy, generous woman. "She gave me life" (*Martin Eden*, 281), he says gratefully—despite the implied threat of racial and bodily taint.

This unnamed "native" woman seems to function in *Martin Eden* as tropical women often do in imperial fiction—as a tempting, beckoning boundary marker of empire. Such "primitive" women were highly liberating to the western male imagination; they seemed to promise a deliverance from the strict sexual codes imposed on white Christian women. The social historian Anne McClintock describes this effect:

> As European men crossed the dangerous thresholds of their known worlds, they ritualistically feminized borders and boundaries. Female figures were planted like fetishes at the ambiguous points of contact, at the borders and orifices of the contest zone. . . . Cartographers filled the blank seas of their maps with mermaids and sirens. Explorers called unknown lands "virgin" territory. Philosophers veiled "Truth" as female, then fantasized about drawing back the veil. In myriad ways, women served as mediating and threshold figures by means of which men oriented themselves in space, as agents of power and agents of knowledge. (24)

But boundaries and borders also can be danger zones, as is indicated in *Martin Eden* by the Hawaiian woman's leprosy. This was the illness most feared by Euro-Americans as the worst of the "Oriental" diseases—here figured as a threat to white racial purity.

Yet the call of the colonial, even with its gender anxieties and threats to the white male body, lures Martin back to the tropics and away from the effete rot of the white metropole. Martin's fear of alienation and disintegration is deeper than any dread of devolution in "savage" lands. His intensifying fantasy of the tropics projects the Pacific islands "as a last bastion for escape and adventure for the urban traveler. . . . a quick fix to the ennui of city life (Wylie 98-99). The South Seas are thus constituted as a site for the physical and spiritual reinvigoration of the depleted Edwardian male. The Islands function as a site of western remasculinization as well as an untamed frontier free from restrictive Euro-American codes.

Martin's San Francisco ennui is worsened by the suicide of his friend, Russ Brissender, a defeated poet. In despair over Russ' death, Martin summons up a catalyzing and transformative Polynesian vision of

> a coral reef smoking in the white Pacific surges. Next, in the line of breakers, he made out a small canoe, an outrigger canoe. In the stern he saw a young bronzed god in scarlet hip-cloth dipping a flashing paddle. He recognized him. He was Moti, the youngest son of Tati, the chief, and this was Tahiti, and beyond that smoking reef lay the sweet land of Papara and the chief's grass house by the river's mouth. . . . He knew there was singing among the trees and that the maidens were dancing in the moonlight. . . . (*Martin Eden* 410)

Given that Brissenden was dying of consumption and alcoholism, this robust vision of the "natural man" of the tropics implies Martin's longing for male power and sexual indulgence, both of which are missing from his life in urban California. Martin implies that he has prior sexual experience with poor girls in Oakland and with Japanese prostitutes and Polynesian *wahine* in the Pacific. But Martin's gentrification project has cloistered him from physical contact with women. For example, he rejects the advances of Lizzie Connolly, a dark-haired factory worker who adores him and would give herself to him. But her rough hands mark her as a manual laborer, an identity Martin now disowns; he recoils from contact with her as though she were worse than a leper. Martin excludes Lizzie from the idealized bourgeois world he wishes to be part of, and he sends her off to night school to educate herself – he wants her to emulate his own regimen of self-improvement.

The upper-class young woman Martin rejects Lizzie for, Ruth Morse, is a slender, blue-eyed blonde with delicate hands. She is a "paragon of liberal education" for Martin to look up to (McElrath 88). She is also four years older than Martin, which permits him to exalt her as a "spirit, a divinity, a goddess" (*Martin Eden* 35). This age gap and her willingness to tutor him invest Ruth with maternal stature—Martin's mother died when he was 11 (*Martin Eden* 98). Ruth assumes a teaching role with Martin, seeking to sooth his class insecurities and provide him with emotional support. This Oedipal-maternal bond complicates Martin's already transgressive cross-class physical attraction to Ruth. So he deflects his desire and worships her disembodied "star-cool chastity" (*Martin Eden* 95) and unattainability.

Martin takes for granted that Ruth is a virgin. Her lack of carnal experience is essential to Martin's belief in the superiority of upper-class women. Unlike hardened factory girls like Lizzie and domestic drudges like Martin's sister Gertrude, Ruth has not been coarsened by sexual experience, in his imagination. Martin's desexualized fancies about Ruth suggest the unconscious connection he makes between class and a woman's body—and between sexlessness and superiority. He equates upper-class femininity with passivity and cannot even imagine that Ruth has a sex drive. Her body was "a pure and gracious crystallization of her divine essence" (*Martin Eden* 58), he rhapsodizes. His longing to be worthy of her "ethereal" essence (*Martin Eden*, 35, 230, 463) drives his project to purge himself. Still, his sublimated dream of "possessing" Ruth sets him "drifting deliciously on a sea of sensibility" (*Martin Eden* 59). This fantasy of immersion with the mother-wife anticipates Martin's orgasmic but solitary plunge into the sea on his Pacific voyage.

Martin's mistake is that he fails to see the real Ruth at all—that is, an attractive young woman whose elegance and poise mask her own self-doubt. His male gaze objectifies and confines her like a songbird (she plays the piano) in a gilded cage. In his eyes Ruth serves as a screen onto which Martin projects his own need for refinement, civility, and culture. In his longing and naivety he does not realize that his spiritualized image of Ruth is an illusion, like the oil painting he examines in the Morse's parlor, a kind of *trompe l'oeil* of class privilege. This picture at first seems to be a three-dimensional depiction of a schooner plowing through heavy seas; but on close inspection Martin discovers that its clever paint-strokes have deceived him into seeing depth and movement where there are none. He dismisses it as a "'trick picture'" (*Martin Eden*, 33) but fails to detect the wider artifice all around him in the Morse home.

Perhaps the image of the ship at sea is a foreshadowing of Martin's troubled last voyage. Perhaps it anticipates Martin's future literary technique as a writer who can make fiction seem real, which Martin terms "a skillful trick" (*Martin Eden* 284). What is certain is that Martin fails to perceive his own delusions of upward mobility and American "success" as he projects them onto Ruth's wan form, itself a kind of *trompe l'oeil*. Martin is right in that Ruth is a virgin. But at this point in the novel she is less a beatified spirit than a frail, perhaps neurasthenic young woman given to headaches and fainting spells (*Martin Eden* 218, 222). The young woman in Oakland on whom London partly modeled Ruth, Mabel Applegarth, was consumptive and often convalescent (Stasz, *Jack London's Women* 42-43). Martin envisions Ruth as an angel in white, yet her pallor conceals an urgent feminine need he cannot detect.

Ruth sexually objectifies Martin at first sight in the Morse parlor when she frames him in her female gaze: "in Martin she sees sex itself" (Whitson 136). From their initial meeting Ruth fixates like a female vampire on Martin's broad neck, corded with muscles and scars (*Martin Eden*, 36, 42, 53, 94, 120, 220, 226). For her it is an unconscious sign of male sexuality. Nothing in her sheltered life has prepared her for Martin's allure, symbolized by his "massive, phallic" throat and neck (DeGuzmán and López 113). Ruth's eyes wander down Martin's statuesque body. She gasps silently at the "wanton thought that rushed into her mind. It seemed to her that if she could lay her two hands upon that neck that all its strength and vigor would flow out to her" (*Martin Eden*, 42-3). Ruth's tight focus on Martin's neck concentrates his masculinity into a powerful fusion of blood and semen—according to Ernest Jones, a common association in "vampire" dreams (*On the Nightmare*, 119). Thus, at age 24, Ruth is unsettled for the first time by her instinctual urges. Like Mabel Applegarth, Ruth has been confined within the parlor of her family home and kept "innocent about love and sexuality" (Stasz, *Jack London's Women*, 43). Confused by physical needs she did not know she has, Ruth seeks to drink Martin's carnal power from his neck like an elixir. She senses that "in his swelling, resilient muscles was the primordial vigor of life" (*Martin Eden*, 106), a cure for her languor. His sexualized aura "seemed to enter into her body and course through her veins in a liquid glow, and to set her quivering with its imparted strength" (*Martin Eden*, 120). She is warmed by "Martin's intensity of power, the old excess of strength that seemed to pour from his body and on and over her" (*Martin Eden* 170). Martin is Ruth's wet dream.

Thus, Ruth and Martin both seek a new self in each other. Ruth is awakening physically, but Martin is blind to her sexual appetite because of his own need to sanctify her as an agent of his own purification. However, to spiritualize Ruth means that Martin has to sublimate his sexual appetite; he fantasizes that his yearning for Ruth is a Romantic "desire to taste divinity" (*Martin Eden* 169). More honestly, on a hot day in the East Bay hills, he admits to her, "'I am more hungry for you than food'" (*Martin Eden* 328), admitting to his own carnal appetite. He says his dream is to lie on her breast forever— surely a desire to "possess" the sexual Oedipal mother, if not an overt vampire dream of Martin's own. Far more directly than Martin, however, Ruth feels the chemistry of physical attraction "that flowed [from him] through her and kindled a kindred warmth" (*Martin Eden* 95) in her. Her fantasies are plainly of sexual intercourse with Martin as her "wanton instincts urged her to throw wide her portals and bid the deliciously strange visitor to enter in" (*Martin Eden* 171).

Yet Ruth stifles her desire even as she stimulates it. Sex to her is still a forbidden expression of physical longing. She relies on the repressive decorum of class to maintain her virginity until Martin can provide her with the respectability of marriage. Like raw clay, she intends to mold "him into the image of her ideal of man" (*Martin Eden*, 123), meaning a bourgeois husband like her father, a corporate lawyer. While Ruth wants to collar Martin's masculinity, her parents want to get rid of him. They regard Martin as a penniless tramp and gold-digger. Her mother also worries about Martin's previous relations with women who are not "'clean.'" She warns Ruth that his contact with colonized women has exposed him to venereal disease and made him a eugenics risk for reproduction (*Martin Eden* 214). In fact Mrs. Morse wants it both ways: she wants Martin to awaken Ruth to the mating urge but encourages Ruth to have a more appropriate man gratify it.

Ruth is both attracted and repelled by Martin's prior sexual experience with Pacific women from Mexico to Japan. She discards her mother's warning and kisses Martin passionately. Ruth melts into his embrace, "and exultantly she reached up and placed both hands upon Martin Eden's sunburnt neck. . . . uttered a low moan . . .and lay half-swooning in his arms" (*Martin Eden* 226). Ruth has become aware of her ability to arouse a man and savors her new-found capacity to feel sexual desire: "She thrilled with these proofs of her power that proclaimed her a woman, and she took an Eve-like delight in tormenting him and playing with him" (*Martin Eden*, 217). After this sensual encounter they become engaged, with the understanding that Martin must become financially secure before they can marry. But after two years of struggle he exhausts himself and feels growing resentment against upper-class privilege, which Ruth comes to represent—and which seems to Martin more a matter of luck than merit. Ruth reins in her passion and ends their engagement. She is pressured by her parents, who worry that she is now past 26; there is no time to lose in finding an appropriate mate. For her part, Ruth mistakenly believes Martin is turning into a socialist—and thus becoming a threat to her class privilege (actually, he is an anti-socialist).

During their many months of sexual abstinence, Martin accepted Ruth's restraint for reasons of his own. He is counting on Ruth's chastity to refine him. On a picnic, when Ruth's lips become stained red from eating cherries, Martin reaches the startling "discovery that she is capable of sexual desire" (Watson, *Jack London*, 147). But Ruth never becomes eroticized in Martin's eyes "in the way of his old careless life" (London, *Martin Eden*, 139) in the arms of colonized women. His epiphany is based on an actual encounter between London and Mabel Applegarth, when her lips were stained by cherries; Jack's initial elation over discovering Mabel's physicality turned to disillusionment over the loss of her Keatsian immortality (Watson, *Jack London*, 272n14). Indeed, Martin likes Ruth better as a bloodless, wraith-like, "*lily-pale spirit* [London's italics]" (*Martin Eden* 52) than as a young woman with reddened lips beginning to discover her sexuality. Similarly, Martin fundamentally misunderstands what Ruth sees in him. He only thinks of himself as a project for Ruth to inspire and uplift, an expression of the maternal role he assigns her. He does not see her red-stained lips as a sign of her appetite for heterosexual experience and female adulthood. He thus fails to apprehend Ruth's physical longing for him. Although it is Ruth who breaks off their relationship, Martin gives up on it too. They both misunderstand each other's wants and work at cross-purposes.

When Martin becomes an overnight success and makes a hundred thousand dollars on his first book, Ruth tries "desperately" (*Martin Eden* 463) to win him back. She risks her reputation by sneaking into his San Francisco hotel room, where she offers her body as proof that she still carries a torch for him. Ruth hugs his neck in her old way and caresses him with increasing abandon. However, after years of dreaming of lying in her arms for "an eon or so" (*Martin Eden* 328), Martin has lost his desire. Martin admits he is "'a sick man'" (464), apparently impotent, barely alive. He is past all sensation and just feels blank—probably a male defense mechanism to ward off performance anxiety about sex with an upper-class white woman. Perhaps the "purity, and saintliness" (*Martin Eden*, 230) Martin has projected onto Ruth's pale body are only attributes of the sexlessness he seeks for himself in his exalted new role as an intellectual. Although Ruth lies yielding in his arms, he lectures her about class prejudice and peer pressure. Ruth counters that she is beyond all convention and has turned "traitor" to bourgeois propriety; she sheds all inhibition and offers herself to him "in free love" (*Martin Eden* 464-5). When Martin holds back, she rises in need and anger. "'I am waiting . . . for you to accept me. Look at me,'" she demands.

Ruth calls on Martin to stop regarding her as an icon of maternal refinement and see her as a young woman ready to enter physical maturity. In this hotel scene she is anything but "'that pale, shriveled, female thing'" scorned by the misogynist poet Brissenden (*Martin Eden* 345). She refuses the role of the nurturing Oedipal mother that Martin has assigned her. In the discourse of feminist psychoanalysis, Ruth instead takes on the part the erotic Oedipal mother—a "disturbingly seductive and aggressive" force (Sprengnether 220). Martin is unprepared for her role reversal and determined to repress and contain Ruth's emerging sexuality. He ignores her passionate appeal and walks her out of the building—as if she were a bundle of laundry *(Martin Eden* 457). Martin's silencing of Ruth is a keystone of his life-denying project of renunciation. For her part Ruth is "stunned" (466) by Martin's rejection.

Ruth was as unprepared for Martin's transformation into sexual impotence as he was for hers into sexual assertiveness. She did not anticipate that, following Martin's literary and financial ascent, he had now come to see "himself as being superior to Ruth in every possible way" (Anderson 11). Martin regrets his own former abjection before Ruth; now he makes her feel inadequate. She did not expect that he would associate class privilege with access to white women's bodies and target hers for his resentment and renunciation. His refusal to make love causes a deep injury, part of his hostile intent to make her feel inferior. Thus, Ruth experiences both sexual arousal and refusal in this traumatic encounter. The presence of her brother outside the hotel suggests that her family pushed her back to Martin. So Ruth is caught between her manipulative parents and her embittered former suitor, and she suffers abjection and humiliation—internal wounds that Martin himself has known. But Martin pays an even steeper price for his rejection of Ruth's body and the social acceptance that marrying into the Morse family would represent.

Martin is not self-aware enough to understand that he has become trapped in the western dilemma of binarism. His "crippling 'double consciousness'" (Reesman 211) submits him to the urban predicament of seeing only class, race, and gender alienation, with no direction home. He can perceive white women only as pure or impure, and their bodies must either be angelic or soiled. He cannot merge his dual images of Ruth as the passive, self-effacing mother and the seductive, self-asserting mother. He can find no resolution in the modern industrial city to this split projection. Neither socialism nor capitalism appeals to him, and his antiquated philosophy of Nietzschean individualism proves inadequate. Oddly, Martin as a writer does manage "to transcend perceived oppositions between critical and commercial acclaim" (Gair, *Complicity*, 132); but he gives himself no credit for it. By the last part of the novel the two main women in his life simply change places, yet he still he cannot form an integrated perspective. Ruth is repudiated as a succubus who would drain him dry to feed her needs, and Lizzie is exalted a selfless martyr who would lose herself to save him. Martin's double identity as both roustabout and writer becomes untenable, his moral compass reverses itself, and his isolation crushes him.

In his confusion and failure to form a viable identity, Martin turns to the discourse of colonialism to find direction. It calls him away from the sick paralysis of the metropole and toward the cure of racialized and gendered male license in the tropics. The call of the colonial thus involves sexual novelty and sensation-seeking—quite different from the frigid call of the Klondike. As a young sailor in the Pacific, Martin had known "full-bodied, South-Sea-Island women, flower-crowned and brown-skinned" (*Martin Eden* 36). Now he believes he can mend his divided self only through tropical sexual healing. He decides to cash in on his new-found success as an author and become an urban wayfarer in the South Seas, attended by indigenous servants. He resolves to settle in French Polynesia, which includes the Society Islands and the Marquesas Islands. Both archipelagoes were visited by London in 1907-08, following in the footsteps of Herman Melville; both authors were in search of the South Pacific "primitive." The valley Martin intends to buy in the Marquesas is "virgin" land, open to his imperial penetration. A panorama of islands and peoples to exploit unfolds in his eager imagination. In the vision he limns below, the tropics are "feminized and spatially spread for male exploration, then reassembled and deployed in the interests of massive imperial power" (McClintock 23). Martin's idea of regeneration is colonial exploring and resource extraction, conducted from his port on Nuku Hiva in the Marquesas:

> The bay, as he remembered it, was magnificent with water deep enough to accommodate the largest vessel afloat, and so safe that the South Pacific Directory recommended it as the best careening place for ships for hundreds of miles around. He would buy a schooner —one of those yacht-like, coppered crafts that sailed like witches—and go trading copra and pearling among the islands. He would make the valley and the bay his headquarters. He would build a patriarchal grass house like Tati's, and have it and the valley and the schooner filled with dark-skinned servitors. He would entertain there the factor of Taiohae, captains of wandering traders, and all the best of the South Pacific riffraff. He would keep open house and entertain like a prince. (*Martin Eden* 420)

Thus, even though he acknowledges a preexisting indigenous social arrangement of authority and power in Polynesia under chiefs like Tati, Martin intends to overthrow it, make himself prince, and construct an imperial regime upon it. Yet he never arrives there. His "instinct of preservation" (474) falters aboard the steamship *Mariposa*, westbound to the Marquesas and Tahiti. The real-life *Mariposa* had carried Jack and Charmian from Pape'ete to

San Francisco and back in early 1908, when she wrote in her diaries that her husband was depressed, drinking too much, and neglecting to work on the manuscript of *Martin Eden* (Watson, *Novels*, 270n8). Withdrawn in his stateroom on the *Mariposa*, Martin takes no pleasure either. He fits in neither with the rough sailors in the forecastle nor the well-heeled guests alongside him at the captain's table. His life remains a paradox that resists solution. The exotic call of the colonial goes silent in the mid-Pacific and leaves him depressed beyond words. He reads Swinburne's "The Garden of Proserpine," a depiction of the blighted netherworld, the antithesis of the lush Garden of Eden. No doubt Martin savors the irony, as it was Ruth who introduced him to Swinburne's poetry during his first magical visit to her home. These desolate verses turn Martin's thoughts to suicide. London's point is plain: Eden is now a dead garden. Martin is a desensitized Adam whose former vitality has withered: his original sin is his lifelessness. Not even Martin's fantasies of Polynesia's hanging gardens, glimmering bays, and eroticized women can rouse him from his torpor. He stumbles from his bunk and stares down at the water.

On a melancholy impulse Martin turns out his light and slips feet-first through the porthole. He is burned out, exhausted, beat -- a forerunner of the Beat Generation, another innovation of *Martin Eden*. He hangs by his arms and drops into the ocean. He floats briefly in the ship's wake, a thousand miles from land. Predatory *ahi* (or bonita) nip at his pale flesh and remind him that he is yielding himself to the Pacific not as a conqueror but a castaway. But the sea is like an anesthetic, calming him, pulling him under. He turns his back on the world, dives deep, and swims down as hard as he can. After his long descent, his lungs explode in a long-pent phosphorescent burst. Suddenly, he is bathed in internal brightness; a kind of lighthouse "inside his brain" flashes an intense white light. Martin tumbles deeper while the light fades, as though he is "falling down a vast and interminable stairway." His head erupts in a kaleidoscopic dazzle of "colors and radiances." Then Martin's South Pacific dream goes black, and he blanks out forever. London's conclusion to *Martin Eden* is literally breathtaking, "one of the finest endings of any American novel" (Kingman 184).

Martin's suicide is orgasmic but solitary; his naked body is "a white statue" plunging through "a milky froth of water" (*Martin Eden* 480-81). Thus, only alone can he experience the sexual release "that he withholds from Ruth" in San Francisco (DeGuzmán and López, 116). Martin once regarded her as unattainable; he saw in her eyes the remote Pacific Ocean at night, "under a full moon, the huge seas glinting coldly in the moonlight" (*Martin Eden* 281). So Martin's long dive is also a simulation of sexual union with Ruth, rolling in the deep and "floating languidly in a sea of dreamy vision" (*Martin Eden* 482). But this is not the ecstatic male experience he had expected to attain in the feminized bays and furrows of glittering French Polynesia. Instead, Martin's downbound Pacific voyage ends in complete darkness. He fails to establish the triumphant new imperial self he once projected in the eager "empery of his mind" (56).

Martin's fantasy of the Pacific Islands as a realm of sunny abundance and fertility mirrored Jack London's excited response to Hawai'i during the first leg of *Snark* voyage, when he wrote much of *Martin Eden*. However, the consolidation of western masculinity that both Jack London and Martin Eden intended to achieve in the Pacific was not gained. It lay at too great a psychological distance, even in the imperial age of steamships like the *Mariposa*. Unlike the narrative of mastery that London created out of his harsh Klondike experience, his Pacific story unraveled into sickness and disillusionment. These conditions worsened after he sailed out of Polynesia into the Melanesian Pacific, from Fiji on to the Solomon Islands. Similarly, Martin's dissolution of selfhood began in Oakland and accelerated on the Pacific; the lure of the tropics could not halt his mental collapse. Even so, when Martin sinks to his death, he is still a perfect physical specimen, "a man in a thousand – in ten thousand" (474), a San Francisco physician exclaims. By contrast Jack London wrecked his body in the southwestern Pacific; this was the physical degeneration he had scorned earlier in the Snark voyage as the "wreckage of races" he observed in the tropics (*Snark* 103). Balmy images of the South Seas that Jack recalled and preserved in Martin Eden's imagination were replaced in London's writings by a chaotic picture of the sweltering Pacific as debased and dangerous. In 1909 Jack London at age 33 returned to California from the Solomons in deteriorating health and worsening drug addiction. He was destined to live only a few more years as he succumbed to both the diseases and false cures he encountered in the colonial Pacific. Thus, it was in the gloomy equatorial jungle that the depleted urban traveler encountered the terrifying dissolution of the body that was spared Martin Eden, the sunken white statue.

Works Cited

Anderson, Lisa. "Justice to Ruth Morse: The Devolution of a Character in *Martin Eden*." *The Call: The Magazine of the Jack London Society* 10.1-2 (2008): 11-14.

Castille, Philip. "The Last Phase of the South Sea Slave Trade: Jack London's *Adventure*." *Pacific Studies* 35.3 (December 2012): 325-341.

DeGuzmán, María and Debbie López. "Algebra of Twisted Figures: Transvaluation in *Martin Eden*." In *Jack London: One Hundred Years a Writer*, ed. Sara S. Hodson and Jeanne C. Reesman. San Marino, Calif.: Huntington Library P, 2002, pp 98-122.

Gair, Christopher. *Complicity and Resistance in Jack London's Novels: From Naturalism to Nature*. Lewiston, NY: Edwin Mellen P, 1997.

Jones, Ernest. *On the Nightmare*. London: Hogarth P, 1931.

Kim, Yung Min. "A 'Patriarchal Grass House' of His Own: Jack London's Martin Eden and the Imperial Frontier." *American Literary Realism* 34:1 (2000): 1-17.

Kingman, Russ. *A Pictorial Life of Jack London*. New York: Crown Publishers, 1979.

London, Jack. *Martin Eden*. New York: Penguin, 1984.

_____. *The Voyage of the Snark*. New York: Penguin, 2004.

McClintock, Anne. *Imperial Leather: Race, Gender and Sexuality in the Colonial Context*. New York: Routledge, 1995.

McElrath, Joseph R., Jr. "Jack London's *Martin Eden*: The Multiple Dimensions of a Literary Masterpiece." In *Jack London: One Hundred Years a Writer*, ed Sara S. Hodson and Jeanne C. Reesman. San Marino, Calif.: Huntington Library P, 2002, pp 77-97.

Phillips, Lawrence. *The South Pacific Narratives of Robert Louis Stevenson and Jack London: Race, Class, Imperialism*. New York: Continuum, 2012.

Reesman, Jeanne Campbell. *Jack London's Racial Lives: A Critical Biography*. Athens: U of Georgia P, 2009.

Sinclair, Andrew. "Introduction." *Martin Eden*. New York: Penguin, 1984.

_____. *Jack: A Biography of Jack London*. 1977; New York: Washington Square P, 1979.

Watson, Charles N., Jr. "The Composition of *Martin Eden*." *American Literature*. 53.3 (1981): 397-408.

_____. *The Novels of Jack London: A Reappraisal*. Madison: U of Wisconsin P, 1983.

Whitson, Carolyn. "Fatal Attractions: Cross-Class Romances in the Working-Class Novels of London, Chute, and Smedley." In *The Image of Class in Literature, Media, and Society*, ed. Will Wright and Steven Kaplan. Pueblo, Colo.: University of Southern Colorado, 1998.

Wylie, Lesley. *Colonial Tropes and Postcolonial Tricks: Rewriting the Tropics in the* novella de la selva. Liverpool: Liverpool UP, 2009.

"The Young Person's Guide" to *Moonrise Kingdom*: Wes Anderson's Theme and Variations on a Theme and Variations of Benjamin Britten

Todd Giles[A]

As is the case with most of Wes Anderson's films to date, *Moonrise Kingdom* (2012) explores the trials and tribulations of trying to hold onto one's innocence in a world of surrogate families and estranged or deceased parents. One of the ways Anderson accentuates this theme is through his choice of music both within and outside of his films. Indeed, one might argue that Anderson is seemingly able to hold on to his own childhood (and those of us who were born in the late 60s and early 70s) by making his presence as the director aurally and visibly felt on the screen through his diegetic and extradiegetic musical choices. As with *The Royal Tenenbaums* (2001) and *The Life Aquatic* (2004), *Moonrise Kingdom* deconstructs the fourth wall by experimenting with what music can and should do in the medium. Even more than his earlier films, *Moonrise* utilizes music to frame the story's action in both subtle and obvious ways. In the latter sense, *Moonrise* is narratively framed around two children's works by British composer Benjamin Britten: *The Young Person's Guide to the Orchestra* (1946) and *Noye's Fludde* (1958).

This musical framing is hard to miss as the film opens and closes diegetically with the beginning and ending narration of *The Young Person's Guide*, and the genesis of the action centers around the flashback to a performance of *Noye's Fludde* a year earlier—and the cancellation of its performance a year later by an actual flood during the film's climax. Much more subtly, though, Anderson mimetically structures the plot of *Moonrise* around the program of *The Young Person's Guide* itself, in which listeners are introduced to the four families of instruments—woodwinds, brass, strings, and percussion—playing variations on an earlier theme. *Moonrise*'s theme, or recurring "melody," if you will, like the four "families" of instruments *The Young Person's Guide* breaks down and then reassembles, is seen in the four surrogate families our young hero, Sam Shakusky, tries to establish throughout the film: with his foster parents, with the Khaki Scouts, with his love interest, Suzy Bishop, and with his future foster-father, Captain Sharp. What links these four families together are a series of "variations" in the form of an escape motif from one family to the next, as each is subsequently introduced,

---

[A] Midwestern State University

played out, and brought together at the end, as is the case with *The Young Person's Guide*, in a full-ensemble fugue.

Two further Britten compositions are included in *Moonrise* in the form of extradiegetic selections from *A Midsummer Night's Dream* ("On the Ground, Sleep Sound") [1960] and *Friday Afternoons* ("Cuckoo!") [1935], both of which add extra layers to the film's narrative progression, as well as diegetic-turned-extradiegetic music from Franz Shubert and Hank Williams, and diegetic selections from Camile Saint-Saens's *Le Carnaval de Animaux* and Mozart's *Cosi fan Tutti*. "Britten is the big one," though, according to Anderson. "The other music to me is stuff on the side," he says, "but Britten is what the movie is sort of built on. I was in *Noye's Fludde* when I was eight years old, nine years old, and loved that music. I've always been interested in Britten, and it happens that he's written and made quite a number of pieces that are expressly for children, so that was sort of what I built from the sound of the movie—the world of it" (Pinkerton 19). In an interview with NPR's Terry Gross, Anderson also says, "I kind of connect to this period that the movie is set in, which is classical pieces that are meant to have an audience of children but that are not written down to children that are meant to kind of educate children in what classical music really is. Britten seemed very motivated by that."

Britten composed *Variations and Fugue on a Theme of Purcell* in the fall of 1946 for Crown Film Unit's educational film titled *The Instruments of the Orchestra*. Britten's friend, Eric Crozier, provided the spoken word accompaniment. The work, better known by its truncated name, *The Young Peron's Guide to the Orchestra*, was first performed on October 15, 1946 by the Liverpool Philharmonic Orchestra. Britten dedicated it to the children of his friends John and Jean Maud, for their "edification & entertainment" (Headington 82-83). *The Young Person's Guide* is based on the Rondeau from Purcell's incidental music to *Abdelazer* by Aphra Behn. Britten's work opens with the theme played by the entire orchestra, followed by variations played by each family of instruments, starting with the woodwinds, then the brass, strings, and finally the percussion. Each variation further allows the instrumental families to highlight each individual instrument in turn. Once the entire orchestra has been introduced, the orchestra is brought back together with the original fugue beginning again with the piccolo, followed by each family in the same order the work began. It comes to a conclusion with a return to Purcell's original melody. Britten opens with an earlier Purcell melody just as Anderson opens with Britten's earlier theme and variations. Indeed, both the orchestral work and Anderson's film have narrators who direct us through the plot of each narrative.

Eleven years after the first performance of *The Young Person's Guide*, Eric Cozier gave Britten a copy of the 16th century "Chester Miracle play *Noye's Fludde* . . . [which] gives a colorful account of the 'flood' story with more than a sprinkling of humor in the persons of the formidable Mrs. Noye and her bibulous friends" (Headington 119). *Noye's Fludde* was first performed at the Aldeburgh Festival in Orford Church on June 18, 1958. As in *Moonrise*, Britten chose a religious venue due to the play's original association with the church. Likewise, amateur performers are cast following the medieval precedent. In the liner notes to the soundtrack, Anderson tells us that "[t]he members of the chorus are the animals on Noah's ark. My friend Sanjay and I played a pair of otters, and my older brother sang an elk. This was in 1979 at St. Francis Episcopal Day School, 345 Piney Point Road, Houston, Texas, 77024. I remember the full details and zip code because there was a poster contest each year for our school book fair, and that was the key information you had to get across" (CD). While the larger, more intricate framing of the film is structured around the four-families theme and variations of *The Young Person's Guide*, the genesis of Sam and Suzy's story centers around the island's annual performance of *Noye's Fludde*.

Moonrise Kingdom is set on the isle of New Penzance off of New Port, Rhode Island from September 1964 to October 1966. For his fictional locale, Anderson plays off of British composers Gilbert and Sullivan's famous comic opera *The Pirates of Penzance* (1879), whose action revolves around a group of orphan pirates who are chased by the Sergeant of Police because the daughter of the Major-General almost weds one of their band. Likewise, Sam, the young canoeing orphan of *Moonrise Kingdom* played by Jared Gilman, is himself chased by the police chief for "wedding" the daughter of one of the island's most prominent families, the Bishops.

Unlike most of Anderson's films in which the time period is not absolutely clear and in which the contemporaneous is often confused due to the musical score—or the music the characters are themselves listening to—*Moonrise* is set during a very specific historical moment in American history. According to Anderson, Suzy, who is played by Kara Hayward, is "bound to end up at Berkeley or something and [Sam is] probably going to get sent to Vietnam [sic] maybe he's going to just miss it. That's the culture they're about to head into" (Pinkerton 18). Along these lines, we learn in the first few minutes of the film that Suzy's family's home is dubbed "Summer's End," hinting at the loss of innocence she and Sam will experience as the film progresses, a loss also mirrored in her mother's admission of infidelity with Captain Sharp, and the latter's intentional loss of bachelorhood when he adopts young Sam during the film's conclusion.

The opening scene (or set) is replete with intertextual references highlighting the fact that what we are watching is a fully imagined universe. Anderson presents the Bishop home as a meticulously balanced stage set as he does in the opening scene of *The Royal Tenenbaums*'s New York brownstone (2001) and Steve Zissou's working meta-model of the *Belefonte*

(2004). The film's aesthetic rationale is one of framing, balance, and toned-down colors, characteristics related not just to aesthetics, but also to the American culture in which the movie is set; a culture on the verge of the explosion of colors, morés, sounds, and freedoms of the late 1960s. One might argue, then, that Britten and Anderson's works also share a nostalgia for earlier, better times—Britten's written just after World War II, Anderson's looking back to a time of seeming American "innocence" before the socio-cultural-political developments of the radical 1960s. Indeed, both *Moonrise Kingdom* and *The Young Person's Guide* carry *en memorium* dedications to youth.[1]

Throughout the first few minutes of the film we are witness to the major recurrent theme in Anderson's oeuvre: the fragmented family unit. According to contemporary American novelist Michael Chabon, "Anderson—who has suggested that the breakup of his parents' marriage was a defining experience of his life—adopts a Nabokovian procedure with the families or quasi families at the heart of all his films, from *Rushmore* forward, creating a series of scale-model households that . . . intensify our experience of brokenness and loss by compressing them" (23). Within the first minute of the film we see both a painting of the house within the house and a small children's toy playhouse sitting on the floor.

Moonrise opens in darkness with ambient sound. Within a few seconds we see an Anderson hallmark—a frame-within-the-frame—in the form of a primitive painting of the house on the wall within which it hangs. Outside thunder rumbles, indicating some kind of trouble in the household as the camera, and thus our own gaze, rests briefly on the painting. To the left are Suzy's "leftie" scissors which will play a pivotal role later in the story; her red plaid attaché hangs on the right. As the camera pans right, we see the portable record player that will momentarily present the music which opens and closes the film. The camera once again briefly comes to rest in the hall as Lionel, one of Suzy's younger brothers, climbs the stairs with his morning bowl of breakfast. He disappears from view for a moment and returns with the record player in hand as he walks to the music room.

The first movement of the film now introduces the family with the aid of music in much the same way that Britten introduces the four instrumental families with the aid of language. Lionel sits on the floor and plays the record, which begins with the voice of a young narrator explaining to both the

---

[1] *The Young Person's Guide* is dedicated to Pamela Maud, one of John and Jean Maud's children who died five years earlier. Anderson's dedication is to David S. Anderson, "For his enthusiastic encouragement and generosity—and his invaluable scouting guidance" (Headington 82-83).

characters in the film and those watching it that

> [i]n order to show how a big symphony orchestra is put together, Benjamin Britten has written a big piece of music, which is made up of smaller pieces that show you all the separate parts of the orchestra. These smaller pieces are called variations, which means different ways of playing the same tune. First of all he lets us hear the tune or the theme, which is a beautiful melody by the much older British composer Henry Purcell.

As soon as the record begins—as if orchestrating the bringing together of the siblings—the camera spins forty-five degrees to the hallway where his brothers Murray and Rudy come out of their rooms in turn as they go to sit around the record player. Another forty-five degrees finds Suzy walking down the attic stairs holding her cat, entering a small room with a piano painted the same orange-red as her dress (also seen in one of the lamp shades across the room). She grabs her binoculars and joins her brothers in the other room. Perched above and behind her brothers on a window seat (we will see her perched atop the stage set dressed as a raven in *Noye's Fludde* later), Suzy briefly opens one of her stolen library books, *Shelly and the Secret Universe*, hinting at her own "secret universe" as she lifts her binoculars to peer out the window atop the third floor. When she does so, the sonic level of the music changes from being inside the movie—that is, from playing inside the house— to becoming the film's score. As the camera pans further back, we get a view of the house, its property, and the water it overlooks. We see, then, a real-life shot of the replica we just saw hanging on the wall.

The camera then cuts, during a slight pause in Britten's work, back inside the house to the boys playing jacks on the floor. As it does, the music once again goes from extradiegetic to diegetic. Panning right, we briefly see Mr. and Mrs. Bishop seated next to one another in their respective offices, a wall separating them. Other than the opening thunder clap, it is not until Suzy appears angled out of the right corner of the first floor kitchen (with mother in the middle ground, father in the background) that we know something is awry with the otherwise perfectly balanced (and tonally muted) Bishop household. That, and the fact that her parents never appear in the same room, much less speak to one another as the camera pans through the house. Indeed, there is always at least one wall separating the couple as the camera pans though the set. Laura Bishop, Suzy's mother (played by Frances McDermand) sits with her legs atop her desk while filing her nails; her father, Walt, (played by Bill Murray) is seated just feet away, but a room apart, reading the newspaper at his own desk. Continuing across the floor, we see the bike that Mrs. Bishop will soon ride to see her lover, Captain Sharp, played by Bruce Willis. The camera stops in front of Suzy, who has moved between her earlier look outside when the camera panned outside of the house, as she looks out what we assume is another window, while at the same time peering directly into the audience, a strategy Anderson similarly used in *The Royal Tenenbaums* when introducing the characters looking at themselves in mirrors, behind which the viewers are situated.

As the camera continues to pan through the rooms and floors of the house while the music continues, sounding slightly different depending on where in the house we are, we eventually come to a narrow hallway, and, if privy to a pause button while viewing the film, we get another taste of Anderson's intertextual self-referencing that works similarly to the way he employs music in this and other films. Passing too quickly through the hall to tell what the small framed pictures on the wall depict, if paused, we see two more primitive paintings, these of future locations in the movie: island's lighthouse and phone station, and Fort Lebanon, which appears toward the end of the film. As the pan continues, the camera momentarily rests on a tight shot of the boys eating breakfast around the kitchen table; behind one is another metatextual image, that of Jack's Church at nighttime, a setting we will visit two more times throughout the film—both of which are key to the development of the plot.

The music continues (we are now just four minutes into the film) as Suzy walks out the front door, storm clouds gone, with a box under her arm and binoculars still around her neck. Was she looking for the mailman, who, as we will learn shortly, arrives by plane? Suzy goes to the mailbox, which has "Summer's End" spelled out in hardware store letters, and retrieves a letter addressed to her from "Sam Shakusky / in care of / Billingsley Boy's Home." In another bit of meta-referencing, we see that the letter, which was mailed August 28th at 4:00 p.m. from Chesterfield Station—two days prior—is posted with a stamp showing a picture of Scout Leader Pierce (played by Harvey Keitel) in his uniform. This exact image will appear briefly in a scouting magazine in the next movement. Suzy reads the letter, to which we are not privy—we know only from whom it was sent—and looks directly at the viewer, perfectly in sync with the whole orchestra coming in to complete the work, before folding Sam's letter and placing it in the box marked "Private" she carried outside with her. The first movement of the film comes to an end with a cut inside to her brother removing the needle from the record, the music once again diegetic.

Not only does Anderson experiment with music which sheds light on plot content and music that is both inside and outside of the action, he also experiments with how that music acts as a framing devise leading into and out of scenes. Music (and other sounds) often overlap scenes before the actual settings change. For example, we hear the beginning of Britten's *Noye's Fludde* (performed one year earlier) while Sam and Suzy are looking at one another in the field the first time they have met in person since the previous year's performance at St. Jack's Church. Here the music acts both diegetically and extradiegetically; they are individually recalling the music in their minds while we, the viewers, are hearing the music outside of the action, albeit only briefly.

The second movement of the film, which lasts less than a minute, opens immediately after the removal of the needle from the record, with Britten's "Playful Pizzicato" from the *Simple Symphony* (1934) taking the extradiegetic role. The music, which is light and plucky, introduces us to the film's narrator, played by Bob Balaban. This is the only Anderson film to date which has a character-narrator who engages both the audience and the other characters in the film a la the Stage Manager from *Our Town*. The narrator not only engages the other characters, he also has the ability to predict the future and move back and forth through time. For instance, in this short movement the narrator points to the plane which is about to land and deliver the mail (which Suzy has already received in the previous scene) and tells us before the fact that Black Beacon Sound, where he is standing in the last scene of the movement, is "famous for the ferocious and well-documented storm which will strike . . . in three days' time." This is the same storm that causes the climax of the film. As with the opening scene, each shot is impeccably framed with a perfectly balanced background, only now, as with the shot of Suzy cropping in from an odd angle in the pantry, the narrator is himself situated in odd places in the frame. There are seven rapid cuts in this movement, each finding the narrator making a brief statement before moving on to the next one—from a chart room, to a forest, to tidal flats, etc., until he appears in two different shots at the Black Beacon Lighthouse, one, the first full view of him, and two, a wide shot close up with him on the right, the lighthouse on the left; his stocking cap and the top of the lighthouse almost perfectly matched in shape and height. Here Britten's "Playful Pizzicato" ends with a final pluck.

Movement three: cut to Camp Ivanhao, Sam's second foster family, where reveille is being bugled by a Khaki Scout as their day begins. The music then moves from diegetic to extradiegetic, capturing the mood of the morning—drumbeats as Scoutmaster Ward (played by Edward Norton) exits his tent for morning inspections. Once inspections are complete, Ward sits down at their dining table and picks up a copy *Indian Corn*, the local scouting magazine. Our eyes now become the camera as we see a two-second shot of the inside of the magazine from Ward's point of view of an advertisement for the "Fort Lebanon Regional Hullabalo, Summer of 65" on the left page; on the right we see a "Letter from Scout Master-in-Chief" which bears the same photograph of Commander Pierce we saw on the stamp on Suzy's letter. A three-second close up of the article reveals further intertextual self-referencing related to the scene at hand: "'Indolence,'" Commander Pierce begins, 'is a fancy word. . . . When the bugler sounds at reveille, something in our bones wants to keep us to our sleeping bags. Tearing ourselves from our warm tents, each morning we fight our own. . . .'" There the article cuts off as Ward turns the page, the camera panning out to reveal a staged tableau of Michelangelo's *The Last Supper* with everyone seated on the far side to the table as Scout Master Ward notices that there is a Khaki Scout missing from the breakfast table. Sam Shakusky, we learn, "flew the coop" before reveille even blew.

The fourth movement introduces the final two families which make up Sam's orphan orchestra. In a nod to *The Last Picture Show*, Anderson uses diegetic 1950s country music to accompany most of the scenes in which Captain Sharp appears; if Sharp's radio is on, so is Hank Williams. We are first introduced to Captain Sharp right after Scout Master Ward learns of Sam's escape; he is fishing with an older man on the doc upon which the police shack sits. "Take these Chains from My Heart" plays on the radio, highlighting Sharp's soon-to-be explained feelings for Laura Bishop. It is also here that we meet Sam's foster parents, Mr. and Mrs. Billingsley of the Billingsley Foster Family for Boys. In a split-screen phone conversation with Captain Sharp and Scout Master Ward (with Becky, the town's operator listening in), we learn that Mr. and Mrs. Billingsley have decided not to invite Sam back to the home "'because this is only the most recent incident involving Sam's troubles.'" Sam's only option now, according to Social Services (played by Tilda Swinton), whom we will meet in another split-screen phone conversation later in the film, is Juvenile Refuge. It is notable that Social Services is actually the name of Swinton's character; that is, she is a nameless representative for children without their own true lineage.

The Fourth Movement closes, as in Britten's work, when all four "families" have been introduced. What remains in both are a series of variations on the original themes, which, in the case of *Moonrise Kingdom*, is that of Sam's escape from one foster family unit to another. The remainder of the film consists of a series of escapes and chases, with a few peaceful interludes for Sam and Suzy as they pitch camp and have, what is for them, the closest thing to a family life together. The repeated escape theme is seen in Sam's escape from camp (and Suzy's escape from home), their subsequent escape from the pursuing scouts in the woods, Sam's escape from Sharp's trailer (and Suzy's second escape from home with the help of the same scouts who were just hunting the pair), their escape from Camp Lebanon and the flood, their near-death escape from atop the lightning-struck church steeple, and Sam's final "escape" from Suzy's window as the story comes to a happy close.

Britten's music is once again heard playing inside the Bishop household in the forty-five second scene when her parents recognize Suzy's absence. From Act 2 of *A Midsummer Night's Dream*, composed five years earlier in June of 1960, we hear, barely audible, "On the Ground, Sleep Sound," which is precisely what Sam is doing in the previous scene as Suzy reads to him from one of her stolen library books, *The Francine Odyssies*, at their first campsite. The cut to the house occurs immediately after the following lines: "Meanwhile, on the Plains of Tabitha, Francine rested. There would be another time for war." Indeed, that "war" was coming from several fronts for Suzy and Sam.

The action comes to a head with a flood caused by the Black Beacon storm which the narrator warned us about in the Second Movement. As the storm hits, Sam and Suzy escape to St. Jack's Church, where they met a year earlier, and where this year's performance of *Noye's Fludde* has been canceled due to the actual flood which has turned the church into the island's storm shelter. As with the final movement of Britten's *The Young Person's Guide*, all of the "families"—barring the Billingslys—are brought together in a fugue of voices and action. In short, the Khaki Scouts, their leaders, the Bishops, Captain Sharp, Social Services, Sam and Suzy, and a church full of townsfolk huddle against the storm while, leave it to Anderson, several children are listening to a record of Britten's *Noye's Fludde*. Throughout the scene we hear, diegetically barely audible in the background, "The Spacious Firmament on High." Sam and Suzy's final escape nearly ends in a double-suicide as they prepare to leap from on high atop St. Jack's steeple. Once the action moves from inside to outside the church, the music extradiegetically shifts to "Noye, Take Thy Wife Anone," also from *Noye's Fludde*. Captain Sharp intervenes, and with the reluctant approval of Social Services over a walky-talky, becomes Sam's new foster father. Just then, lightning strikes the steeple, obliterating it; Sharp, Sam, and Suzy literally hang from a rope tied to Sharp's ankle, saving them, as the music comes to a crescendo with children singing "Halleluiah. Halleluiah."

The storm, the narrator tells us, was the "region's most destructive meteorological event of the second half of the twentieth century. . . . The coastal areas of New Penzance were battered and changed forever. Mile 3.25 Tidal Inlet [where Sam and Suzy camped before getting caught by her parents and Captain Sharp, and where presumably they had intercourse] was erased from the map." Out of the destruction, though, comes renewal: "harvest yields the following autumn," the narrator tells us, "far exceeded any previously recorded and"—now standing in front of the Bishop's house he informs us that—"the quality of the crops was said to be extraordinary." For Sam and Suzy weathering the storm of their youthful love indeed proved abundant and fruitful.

In the final scene, we return diegetically to the Bishop children listening to the end of *The Young Person's Guide*, Suzy once again perched in her window seat reading from another stolen library book, this one titled *The Return of Auntie Lorraine*; her brothers, now dressed for the day, sprawled out in their same positions on the floor around the record player. The record's narrator explains that "The instruments come in one after the other in the same order as before, beginning with the piccolo." As in the opening scene of the film, the camera pans from the music room to the boy's rooms, to the room in which we first met Suzy, where now sits Sam at his easel. Here the narration of the record is overshadowed by Mr. and Mrs. Bishop calling their children to dinner. As the boys turn off the record, the music returns extradiegetically to Britten's ethereal and innocent "Cuckoo!" from *Friday Afternoons*. Sam, dressed in a junior version of Captain Sharp's Island Police uniform, exits out the same window Suzy peered through as she was presumably looking for the mail plane at the beginning of the film. Adopting the camera eye, we see that the painting on Sam's easel is of Tidal Inlet 3.25, which he and Suzy have named "Moonrise Kingdom."

Perhaps more than any Anderson film to date, *Moonrise Kingdom* seamlessly weaves together the visual and aural to tell a multivalent tale of nostalgia, alienation, and lost individual and national innocence. Anderson's meticulous incorporation of Britten's music—both *as* music and as a sort of aural framing storyboard—provides viewers a heretofore unexperienced richness and complexity that can easily go unnoticed among the film's stunning visuals, clever dialogue, and youthful love story. In an interview with Matt Zoller Seitz, Anderson, in discussing Leonard Bernstein's recoding of *The Young Person's Guide to the Orchestra* used in the film, says, "there's really three composers involved. There's Purcell, whose music Britten took apart and rearranged and made something new out of, and then there's Leonard Bernstein, who's conducting the whole thing, as well as making it into this narrated experience" (313-316). Add to this already multi-leveled authorship Anderson's own authorial voice as he creates a new story based on Bernstein's telling of Britten's retelling of Purcell's musical accompaniment to Behn's *Abdelazer*, and we are left not only with one of Anderson's richest films, but with the benefit of a new generation of young people being introduced to the earlier work of Britten and Purcell.

Works Cited

Anderson, Wes. "Wes Anderson, Creating a Singular 'Kingdom.'" Interview with Terry Gross. *Fresh Air*. Natl. Public Radio. 29 May 29, 2012.

Anderson, Wes. Liner Notes. *Original Sound Track: Moonrise Kingdom*. CD. ABKCO Music and Records, Inc., 2012.

Chabon, Michael. "The Film Worlds of Wes Anderson." *New York Review of Books* 60.4. 7 March 2013: 23.

Headington, Christopher. *Britten*. NY: Holmes and Meir, 1982.

Moonrise Kingdom. Screenplay by Wes Anderson and Roman Coppola. Dir. Wes Anderson. Focus Features, 2012.

Pinkerton, Nick. "An Island of His Own." *Sight & Sound* 22.6 (June 2012): n.p.

Seitz, Matt Zoller. *The Wes Anderson Collection*. New York: Abrams, 2013.

Aw Yeah!
Comics and Popular Culture in the Classroom

Patricia M. Kirtley[A] & William M. Kirtley[B]

Introduction

Cartoons have historically held an advantage in breaking into world popular culture.

(McCloud 42)

Comic books form a vibrant, vital, part of popular culture. Legendary cartoonist, Will Eisner (1917-2005) describes them as "the world's most popular art form" (*Comics* xii). They entertain, inspire, and transport us. They influence our collective imagination and reflect the concerns of the time in which they appear (Duke Library 1). One sees their influence in literature, radio, television, films, and video games.

Eisner explains in *Comics and Sequential Art* that comic books combine the words, images, and layout of artists and writers to weave the fabric of communication (xiv). Comic books involve readers because the characters speak for them and to them. To paraphrase theorist Scott McCloud in *Understanding Comics*, we don't just observe comic books, we become them (36). This process constitutes an interactive sociocultural act.

Some consider comic books lowbrow entertainment. Jules Pfeifer, a cartoonist for the *New Yorker*, describes them as "junk" (Eisner *Contract* xvii). Eisner prefers the term "sequential art." He thinks it would help "to correct the feeling of inferiority by artists and writers in this field" (Library of Quotes). Comics gained a measure of respectability after Art Spiegelman won a Pulitzer Prize for his graphic novel *Maus* in 1992. Today, comic books are the subject of scholarly study in a variety of disciplines.

The text-image format provides creators with a multitude of story options or genres. They run the gamut from webcomics, to graphic novels, to manga. In the past, people looked at comic books as "funnies" meant for children. Jahsonic, a contributor to the Art and Popular Culture website, observes that modern day comics "are not necessarily funny or for children" (1).

Ben Saunders, a professor at the University of Oregon, terms comics

---

[A] Independent Scholar

[B] Central Texas College

"[t]he most effective form of communication ever devised" (cited by Cooper 8). Everything from airline safety cards, to instruction manuals, to *Preventative Maintenance Magazine*, to Eisner's work for the US Army, employs this medium. There is a comic book for people of every age, disposition, and predilection.

This analysis focuses on one comic book in a series written for children. The perspectives gained from such an examination reveal that *Tiny Titans, Welcome to the Treehouse* Vol. 1 encourages and facilitates literacy and opens children's minds to stories that delight and enchant them.

Welcome to the Tiny Titans

> *There's a lot more in cartoons than meets the eye.*
> (McCloud 45)

Welcome to the Treehouse Vol. 1 is a colorful, amusing comic book for all ages, especially young children. Art Baltazar (writer and artist) and Franco Aureliani (writer) won Eisner awards for Best Publication for Kids in 2009, 2011, and 2014. Baltazar self-published his first comic book, *Wolf Boy*. One morning, while feeding his children breakfast, he received a call from Jann Jones, an editor at DC Comics. She asked him to create a comic book series for children. His reply to the offer of a dream job for a cartoonist was, "YES! Possitootly Absolootly!" (Baltazar, Tiny Titans webpage). From then on, Baltazar considered it his job to write comics for six-year-olds. The context of the history of comics and their use in the classrrom helps one better understand the importance of Baltazar and Franco's work.

History of Comic Books

Gene Leung Yang won an Eisner award in 2007 for his graphic novel, *American Born Chinese* (208). He based his 2014 *The Shadow Hero*, on the Green Turtle, the first Asian American superhero. Yang's true-to-history graphic novel is a contender for another Eisner award. Yang discusses the controversy over comic books and children on his webpage "The History of Comic Books in Education."

Yang explains that the employees of Eastern Color Printing Company introduced the first modern comic book in 1933. They collected a number of political cartoons and printed them in book form (1). DC Comics introduced Superman (1938), Batman (1939) and Wonder Woman (1941). This marked the advent of the superhero and ushered in a golden age of comic books. Comic book publishers responded to demand for their product by printing hundreds of issues. Some single-issue comic books sold millions of copies.

Children loved these early comic books. However, many parents, teachers, and librarians remained skeptical, despite the findings of Robert L.

Throndyke, a pioneer in educational research at Columbia Teachers College, who determined the grade level for *Superman* #11 (1940) at 6.6 and *Batman* #8 (1940) at 5.9. He published his results in an article, "Words and Comics" (1941), that appeared in the prestigious *Journal of Experimental Education* in which he concludes that comic books are of "real value" in teaching children to read (112). Subsequently, he co-authored a language arts workbook featuring Superman.

Those who saw little value in comic books found an advocate in Fredric Wertham, a well-known psychiatrist. In his 1953 work, *Seduction of the Innocent*, he argues, "Comic books with their words and expletives in balloons are bad for reading" (10). In the course of interviewing delinquent youths, Wertham found that they all read comic books. He concluded this is what caused their dysfunctional behavior. Wertham gained publicity when he presented his erroneous conclusions to a Senate sub-committee hearing on juvenile delinquency. Subsequently, he serialized them in the 1950s' arbiter of taste, *The Ladies' Home Journal*.

Comic Books and Education

The debate over comic books turned to their use in schools to teach reading. In 1944, Sidonie Gruenberg, a noted child development expert, saw comic books as a force for good, with multiple applications in education. Yang recalls that Nebraska Principal Lucile Rosencrans disagreed, calling comic books a "stumbling block" to learning (1).

Emma Swain, a reading diagnostician, in her 1978 article "Using Comic Books to Teach Reading and Language Arts," notes that "teachers and parents have criticized comic books for years" (1). Swain conducted a survey of 169 students in grades 4 through 12 and found that good students read more comic books than poor students. She pointed out the tremendous popularity of comics. Retailers sold 20 million comic books a month in 1977 (1). She concludes that the demand for comics is an indication of their potential for teaching children reading. She recommends that every classroom have a box of comics for students to read.

Positive appraisals of comic books have flourished in modern times. Author Jennifer Haines, in her 2004 article, "Why Teach with Comics," argues that comic books generally require high reading levels. She insists that it is a grievous mistake to dismiss reading material that is "challenging to read, thoughtful and insightful, and age appropriate," simply because it is a comic book (1).

The mission of school librarians is to support the curriculum and encourage reading. Librarians were originally some of the most vociferous opponents of comic books. Modern librarians have a different view. Carol Tilley, a professor of Library Science at the University of Illinois, in her article,

"For Improving Early Literacy, Comics Is No Child's Play," notes the influence that comics have had on children's literature, especially in the use of frames (panels), speech bubbles (balloons), motion lines, and sound effects (1). (See Appendix A).

Librarian Jane Goodall describes the benefits of using comics in the classroom to readers of the *Guardian* (UK) in her article, "Ten Benefits of Reading Comics." She argues that comic books encourage a love of reading, improve vocabulary, and increase confidence. She believed that comic books prove excellent resources for teaching reluctant and voracious students, as well as those for whom English is a second language (1).

David Jacobs, professor of English at the University of Windsor (CN), in *Graphic Encounters*, states that comic books are effective in teaching print literacy, but more important, multi-modal literacy, which he defines as "the ability to relate something to create meaning with and from texts that operate not only in alphabetic form, but also in some combination of visual, audio, and spatial form as well" (3).

Publisher and pundit Corey Blake in his article, "The Benefits and Risks of Comics in Education," argues that comic books are stronger learning tools than textbooks, able to "combine story and information more effectively than any other medium" (1). As proof he cites two facts: the brain processes pictures 60,000 times faster than text; and humans communicated in pictures before they used words (1).

The arguments against comic books have recently resurfaced. Amanda Hendricks, a recent graduate of the University of California, Chico, (2014) demonstrates in her honors thesis, "Sexism, Female Performativity, and Female Presence in Comics" that D.C. and Marvel Comics have become increasingly violent and sexist over the years.

Koppy McFad, writing for the website, *Comic Book Bin*, charges that these comics were no longer suitable for children (1). Inigo Montoya (Dorkdaddy) concurs. He insists that publishers sell edgy comic books to appeal to a more mature audience that can afford expensive comics. He claims that *Welcome to the Treehouse* is more suitable for young children than modern superhero comics.

Welcome to the Treehouse is a powerful and proven tool for teaching reading. Readers of all abilities identify with the characters and relate to the stories. The images help reluctant readers understand the text and proficient readers use it as a springboard to more advanced reading levels. This comic book is an excellent resource for bilingual education. Teachers of English can use Tiny Titans activity books as an invaluable tool. *Welcome to the Treehouse* is not only helpful in teaching children to read, but is wholesome and appropriate for young children.

It helps to know something about the terms, attributes, and history of comics before attempting to analyze an individual comic book. It is even more important to start thinking like a child. *Welcome to the Treehouse* features those knock-knock jokes that make adults cringe, but results in gales of laughter from kindergarten through third graders who promptly repeat them again and again. For example, "Why are fish so smart?" "Why?" "Because they swim in schools." (Baltazar and Franco 118).

Analysis of *Welcome to the Treehouse*

This is a very silly book, friends.
(Monical, *Goodreads*)

Roland Barthes (1915 – 1980), the French semiotician, establishes an analytical foundation in *Image-Music-Text*, He sees three messages in a visual work of art: a linguistic message in the form of a caption, a denoted message in the image itself, and a connoted message that is the result of the action of the creator and reflection of what society thinks (17). McCloud shows us how to graph transitions in *Understanding Comics* and Hendrix sends us her coding sheets. Richard Jenkins and Debra Detamore provide a math skills graphing activity in *Comics in Your Curriculum*. Bart Beatty, a comic books scholar, continues to to do extensive and valuable statistical research at the University of Calgary.

Comic book fans review Welcome to the Treehouse

The next question is how the comic book community received Baltazar and Franco's bright, lively, and fun comic book. The website *Goodreads* featured 803 community reviews. Most reviewers gave it high marks and some interesting comments were included (Goodreads 1).

"Chuck" couldn't keep track of all the characters. Also there were two Wonder Girls. Reply: This is not a problem for children. Two five and seven-year-old research assistants easily identified all 43 characters after several readings. They noted that there were three Wonder Girls in the DC comic universe and were not in the least bothered by the fact that two of them appeared in *Welcome to the Treehouse*. After all, they wore different outfits.

"Sesana" argued that *Welcome to the Treehouse* was really "much more about kids than super heroes," and that "there's jokes that require some decent backstory" (*Goodreads* 1). Reply: True! No argument here, except to mention that having a DC back-story and continuity with it makes it more fun for kids. The DC universe provides an exciting milieu for young readers, but the focus is on the commonality of childhood experiences.

"Michelle" noted that there was no story line in *Welcome to the Treehouse*. Reply: In contrast to DC comics for more mature readers that feature one story line throughout the entire work, Baltazar and Franco created a series of engaging one to three-page stories to match the short attention span of beginning readers.

"D'Anne" commented, "The female characters are often portrayed in stereotypical 'girly' ways, playing with Barbies and talking about cute boys" (*Goodreads* 1). Reply: Boys romp, play, and have fun in groups. Girls play with Barbie dolls (albeit one is a Batgirl doll), problem solve, cook, help others, babysit, and quite often save the day. Although there is room for improvement in *Welcome to the Treehouse* as far as sexual stereotyping, overall, the creative authors are sensitive to this issue.

Text--captions, background, word balloons, and sound effects

Barthes' first level is about why and how writers present words. He uses the term "linguistic message" to refer to words as meaningful written images. Text answers the question, "What does a character say?" It binds the reader to the character. Text introduces, directs, anchors, and builds the story. In the absence of words, readers rely on their own experiences to understand the story. Comic book artists prove their talent by drawing a story with few words.

The text-image nature of comic books helps children to read. Adults often read comics to pre-school children. This anticipatory preparation encourages them to learn to read. The Flesch-Kincaid grade level scale indicated a 2.5 reading level. Capstone publishers listed the reading level as grades 1 – 2, the interest level as grades 1 – 3, and the Lexile level as 150L (Capstone. com 1). The Lexile level allows teachers to match text with the developmental level of learners. MetaMetrics, the parent company of the Lexile Reading Framework, shared their research with the team that developed the Common Core Standards. Lexile bands (ranges) match Common Core bands. Capstone publishing added a hard cover and library binding to *Treehouse* for sales to schools at a price of $15.95. The Capstone website refers to this work as a graphic novel to avoid the stigma of advocating the use of a comic book in school.

There is a tremendous amount of information in each frame. A sample of 593 words in 75 frames of Baltazar and Franco's *Welcome to the Treehouse* indicate that the average number of words per frame is 7.0. Some of the words reflect everyday speech patterns familiar to children, such as "um no" (13), "Yep!" (13), and contractions like "that's awful" (17).

Certain artistic devices provide emphasis. Nick Napolitanto (letterer issues #1 & 2) and Baltazar (letterer issues #3-6) both favor an upper-case, straightforward lettering style. They use lots of bold type, color, and borders. Eisner favors this type of old-school hand lettering because it is "the most idiosyncratic and expressive means" of expressing the author's emotions

(*Comics* 24).

There are 1986 words in the 470 frames of *Welcome to the Treehouse* (See Appendix B). Seventy-four percent of them are in speech bubbles that carry the action of the story and enable the reader to identify directly with the characters. Fourteen percent of the words are in the background. Sound effects like "POP" (12), "Wwaahh!" (17), and "Swoosh" (51) lend excitement and drama to the story,

Twelve percent of the words are in the captions. Even though captions contain the smallest percentage of words, they are important because they give the reader the title of the story and set the scene. If the reader does not get the joke or understand the story, it is most likely due to missed information given in the first frame. Eisner warns artists that "[t]he most important obstacle to surmount is the tendency of the reader's eye to wander" (*Comics* 41).

Characters – boys, girls, pets, monsters, and adults

Barthes calls the obvious meaning the denoted level (65). The viewer sees polysemous images in the frames of a comic book. Artists call a page with one frame a splash page. If there is no frame, the artist has a reason, perhaps, to indicate unlimited space. The first frame of a story is important. It introduces the plot and characters. A frame is the literary equivalent of a paragraph. McCloud notes that the images within a frame act like adjectives and adverbs (11).

Analysis of the characters depicted in the frames of *Welcome to the Treehouse* (N=470) indicate that Balthazar and Franco do not usually use characters or objects in the background, except to set the scene in the opening frame. The characters act more like children than superheroes. This, much to the dismay of committed DC fans.

The number of girl characters and boy characters is reflective of the DC universe. Boys (39%) outnumber girls (27.4%). The portrayals of cute animals (21.9%) and monsters (6.4%) exceed the portrayals of adults (4.7%) (See Appendix C).

All categories of characters appeal to young boys and girls. Boy and girl characters are equal in their powers and foibles. Children find it amusing that Baltazar and Franco portray so few adults. The parents of two of the Tiny Titans, Rose and Raven, are the principal, Mr. Slade and a substitute teacher, Mr. Trigon, at Sidekick Elementary School. Patterned on evil characters from the DC universe, Baltazar and Franco portray these adults as being mildly annoying or overwhelmingly kind. The two girls comment on their fathers, "This is so embarrassing" (8).

It proved difficult to sort the characters in the world of the Tiny Titans into specific categories. Bee is miniscule, but interacts equally with much larger characters. Rather than put her in the "girl" category or create an "insect" category, the researchers put her in the "animal" category. The comic book writers refer to all monsters as "he." If one included monsters in the "boy" category, it would skew the ratio of boys to girls even further towards the boys. Blue Beetle joined the "boys" because he looks and acts like the other boys. In one story, he brings his collection of bugs to the Pet Club. It was impractical, inaccurate and exhausting to count hundreds of tiny insects and put them in a separate category. As far as Blue Beetle's backpack that speaks in glyphs, well, it is in a category all its own.

Themes – welcome to a child's world

Analysis of Welcome to the Treehouse revealed compelling themes and a signature pattern of transitions between frames. While action comics tend to feature good versus evil conflicts, Baltazar and Franco embraced the reality of a child's milieu in focusing on the themes that dominate their world. Investigation of the total number of frames (N-470) revealed that the seven themes were: relationships (24%), jokes (15%), adults (15%), competition (15%), school (15%), mischief (6%), and pets (3%) (See Appendix D). None of the themes revolve around violence or sexist situations.

The stories in *Welcome to the Treehouse* center on the experiences of primary school students: likes and dislikes, gossip, teasing, and clothes. The character Terra is a good example. Baltazar and Franco modeled her on a DC super hero who has the power of geo-kinesis. Terra throws rocks at Beast Boy, who interprets her actions as a sign that she likes him (The feeling is mutual). Her actions pay homage to a comic that had a great influence on Will Eisner, George Herriman's early 20th century newspaper comic strip, *Krazy Kat.* Herriman's long-running plot revolved around the action of Ignatz, a mouse that "behurdils" (throws) bricks at Krazy Kat who misinterprets this action as a signifier of affection (Cooper, 11).

Every story involves a joke. The humor revolves around knock-knock jokes, running gags, word play, unexpected outcomes, or adults who are slow to grasp a situation. Robin (as Nightwing), Batgirl, and a penguin stand on each others' shoulders, don a Batman mask and cowl, and fool Commissioner Gordon into thinking they are Batman with a cold.

One frame in *Welcome to the Treehouse* depicts an adult figure from his shoulders down, the view as seen by a small child (5). The name of the character is not revealed. One must know the DC backstory to get this joke. Competition takes the form of a game of tag over who gets to use a swing set, a continuing foot race, and dealing with pesky birds. In the latter two contests, a girl wins by outwitting the boys. Several stories are set in Sidekick Elementary School. Beast Boy fools the science teacher by morphing into different animals. Rose's little brother Jericho hypnotizes Mr. Slade, the principal. The

Tiny Titans do get into lots of good-natured trouble. In the story "Penguins in the Batcave," Alfred sits Robin, Beast Boy, Aqualad, and a waddle of penguins in the corner for messing up the Batcave.

Transitions – the construction of sequential reality

A hallmark of excellence is how a comic artist handles the transition between frames. Artists advance the story by leading the viewer past the closure of a gutter. Several comic book scholars have categorized and graphed these leaps of faith. McCloud describes six categories (70-78). The first category, moment-to-moment, depicts a slight change, the wink of a character's eye. His second type of transition is action-to-action. Imagine a baseball in the first frame, and in the second, a baseball player knocks it out of the park. McCloud's third category is subject-to-subject within an overall scene or idea. Watch the runner break the tape in one frame and in the next see a stopwatch recording the time. The fourth type, scene-to-scene, takes the viewer across significant distances of time and space. The fifth type is aspect-to-aspect. This transition depicts various features of a scene. There is no logical relationship between frames in the sixth type of transition, the non-sequitur.

The transitions in Baltazar and Franco's work display the nuances of sophisticated Japanese manga. Out of 470 transitions between frames, 27% were moment-to moment, 57% action-to-action, 6% subject-to-subject, 3% scene-to-scene, 12% aspect-to-aspect, and 0% non-sequitur (See appendix D). Art Baltazar's degree in visual arts from Columbia College of Chicago accounts for much of the sophistication and technical proficiency of his work.

Conclusion

Today the possibilities for comics are – as they always have been – Endless.
McCloud, 212

An analysis of words, characters, themes, and transitions shows that Baltazar and Franco's *Welcome to the Treehouse* is appropriate for beginning readers, is free from sexism and violence, and has a place in the kindergarten through third grade classroom. It offers an exciting, imaginative world that encourages small children and (ESL) English-language learners to independently recognize words while seeing the accompanying humorous cartoons.

Welcome to the Treehouse! Say hello to Robin, Aqualad, Blue Beetle, Raven, and Rose. Visit Sidekick Elementary School. Look out for Mr. Slade and Mr. Trigon, those reformed super villains on the teaching staff. Let's play in the Batcave, climb on the dinosaur, roll the Big Penny, and frolic with bunnies, bats, and birds. Check on who likes whom. Robin likes Batgirl, Beast Boy likes Terra. Catch the race between Speedy and Flash. See who gets dibs on the swings after a game of tag with the Fearsome Five. It's all there in *Tiny Titans:*

Welcome to the Treehouse. It is a bright optimistic comic book that reflects a child's world. Aw yeah! That is truly awesome!

Works Cited

Baltazar, Art (artist, writer and illus. for issues #3-6), Aureliani, Franco. (writer), Napolitano, N. (illus. issues # 1 & 2). *Tiny Titans: Welcome to the Treehouse*. Vol. 1. New York: DC Comics, 2007. Print.

Baltazar, Art, Tiny Titans Webpage, 2014. Web. 1 Mar. 2015.

Barthes, Roland. *Image-Music-Text*. New York: Hill and Wang, 1977. Print.

Blake, Corey. "The Benefits and Risks of Comics in Education." *Comic Book Resources*, 28 July 2014. Web. 5 Feb. 2015.

Capstone Publishers. Recently reviewed products. *Welcome to the Treehouse*, 2014. Web. 6 Feb. 2015.

Cooper, Matt. "Holy Scholarship!" *Cascade, University of Oregon Arts and Sciences*. (Winter 2015): 6-11. Print.

Duke Library. "Comic Book Culture," 2005. Web. 2 Mar. 2015.

Eisner, Will. *A Contract with God*. New York: W.W. Norton and Co., 2006. Print.

---. *Comics and Sequential Art*. New York: W. W. Norton Co., 2008. Print.

---. LibraryofQuotes.com, 2013. Web. 7 Feb. 2015. <http://libraryofquotes.com>

Goodall, Jenna. "10 Benefits of Reading Comics." *Stories with Ms. Jenna*," 2013. Web. 7 Feb. 2015.

Goodreads. *Tiny Titans Vol. 1: Welcome to the Treehouse*, 2013. Web. 2 Feb. 2015.

Haines, Jennifer. "Why Teach with Comics?" *Reading with Pictures*, 2004. Web. 7 Feb. 2015.

Hendricks, Amanda. "Sexism, Female Performativity and Female Presence in Comics." Honors thesis at California State University, Chico, CA., 2014. Print.

Jacobs, David. *Graphic Encounters*. New York: Bloomsbury Academic, 2013. Print

Jahsonic. "Comic Books," *The Art and Culture Encyclopedia*, 2015, 17 Jan. Web. 1 Feb. 2015.

Jenkins, R. (writer and illus.) and Detamore, D. (writer). *Comics in Your Curriculum*. Marion (IL): Pieces of Learning Publishers, 2008. Print.

Lexile Measures and Grade Levels. Web. 1 Mar. 2015.

McCloud, Steve. (w&a). *Understanding Comics*. New York: Harper Collins, 1993. Print.

McFad, Koppy. (2008). "Comics Aren't for Kids Anymore," *Comic Book Bin*, 2008. Web. 1Mar. 2015.

Meconis, Dylan. "How to Write Comics Criticism." Dylan Meconis Website, 2012, 18 Sep. Web. 1 Mar. 2015.

Montoya, Inigo. "Comics Aren't for Kids Anymore." 6 Nov. 2014. Web. 1 Mar. 2015.

Swain, Emma. "Using Comic Books to Teach Reading and Language Arts." *Journal of Reading*. Vol. 22, #3, (December1978): 253-258. Print.

Thorndyke, Robert. "Words and the Comics." *The Journal of Experimental Education*. vol. 10 #2, (Dec. 1941): 110-113. Print.

Tilley, Carol. "For Improving Early Literacy, Reading Comics is No Child's Play." *University of Illinois News*, 2005. Web. 4 Mar. 2015.

Wertham, Fredrick. *Seduction of the Innocent*. New York: Rinehart. 1953. Print.

Yang, Gene. "History of Comic Books in Education." *Comics in Education,* 2003. Web. 1 Mar. 2015.

Yang, Gene. "Strengths of Comics in Education." *Comics in Education*, 2003. Web. 1 Mar. 2015.

Appendix A – Frames, gutter, speech balloon, and caption adapted from Meconis (1).

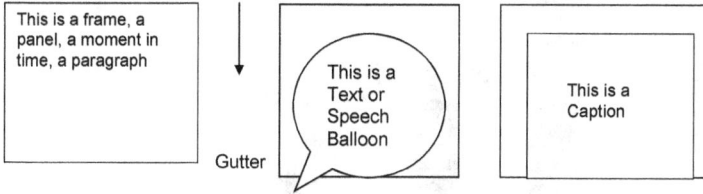

Appendix B - Source of Words in Welcome to the Treehouse, N=1986

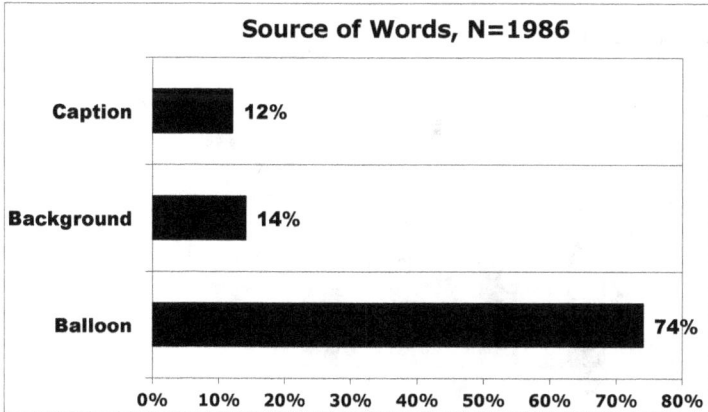

Appendix C - Characters – Number of Appearances, N=1424

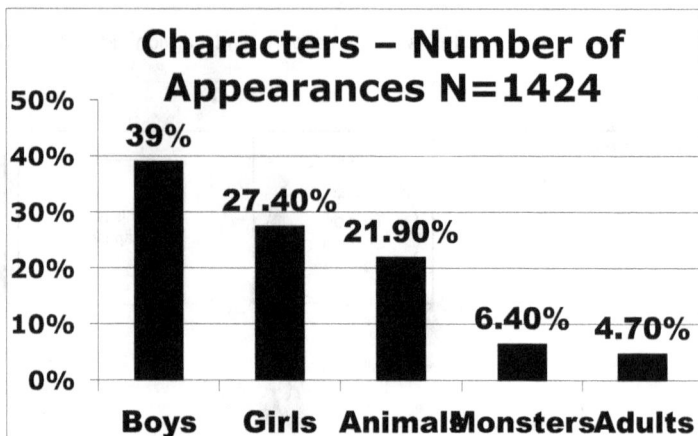

Appendix D - Themes in Welcome to the Treehouse, N=470

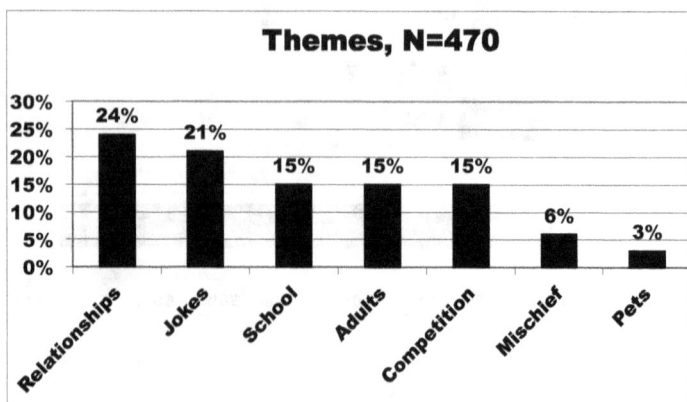

Appendix E – Transitions between frames N=470

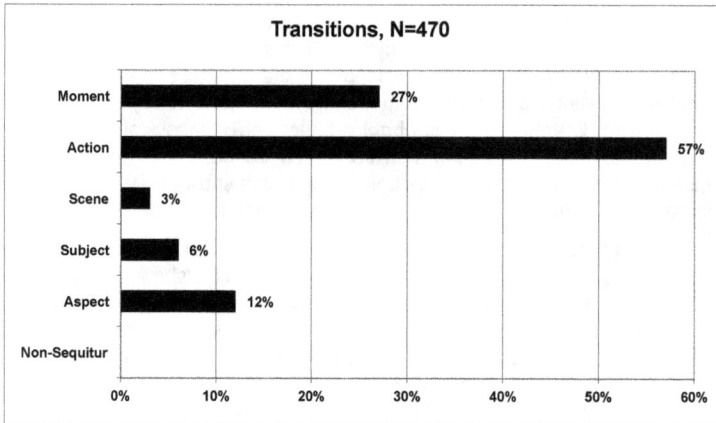

Transitions, N=470

Moment	27%
Action	57%
Scene	3%
Subject	6%
Aspect	12%
Non-Sequitur	

0%   10%   20%   30%   40%   50%   60%

BOOK REVIEWS

Hitchcock à la Carte
By Jan Olsson, Duke University Press, 2015

Romana Guillotte, *University of Nevada, Las Vegas*

"Good evening."

These words started the television show *Alfred Hitchcock Presents* (and the Alfred Hitchcock Hour) by the notorious director himself. In Jan Olsson's *Hitchcock à la Carte*, the length of the director's works, stretching from film, television, and print media are all on the menu, ready for immediate consumption. Olsson's study is about a trifecta of Hitchcockian themes: the macabre, food and the director's own corporeal image. The largest examples of these are drawn from the long-running television show, an hour-long meal, where hors d'oeuvres and murder are served to you by the director.

The study starts chronologically from Hitchcock's arrival in the U.S. in 1937 and, as with his famous silhouette from his television show, Olsson starts with Hitchcock's corporeal image. While the director's more famous film works are discussed at a decent length, the real meat of the book comes with the television show. Episodes specifically sited include "Banquo's Chair" and "Lamb to the Slaughter." In the first, "Banquo's Chair," the main action revolves around an inspector trying to get a confession out of a murderer at a meal the inspector hosts, while "Lamb to the Slaughter" revolves around a pregnant housewife who uses the leg of lamb to kill her cheating husband. While this is a small portion, the other examples he cites are a veritable buffet of macabre delights.

While discussing the director's corporeal image, Olsson pulls from print ads and uses the 'bumpers' - the bits before the episode airs and between commercials – though he never uses this term exactly. In these bumpers, Hitchcock introduces the episode and usually spoofs his image, often with comments on his weight, eating habits, the macabre, and how they all tie into the story of the episode he is presenting. Olsson interviews one of the more prolific writers of the television series, Jimmie Allardice, and picks the writer's brain on the further exploitation of Hitchcock. The use of doubles or a made-up 'brother' appear in several of these bumpers, to which the director's image is then exploded, used as a marionette, tied to railroad tracks, and so much more.

When the section on "English Murders" is served to the reader halfway through the book, it is like a jolt to the senses. The example of domesticity, the huge obstacles to divorce in England, and the fact that guns are not too readily available, Hitchcock noted, often called for more drastic measures that the director also called "artistic" – all the basis for his finely cooked films. Jan Olsson further mentions that the puritan foundations of America are held so closely beneath the cultural surface that cardinal sins, such as gluttony "borderline on pathological." Hitchcock's brand satisfies our hunger for the macabre on this side of the pond.

Jan Olsson definitely has a mind for the analysis of television, a gift even. Even with the bulk of Hitchcock material out there, this fresh perspective gives Hitchcock fans something new to sink their teeth into. Overall, the book is a fine multi-course meal that brings all sorts of new tastes and senses to explore.

Television, Religion, and Supernatural: Hunting Monsters, Finding Gods
By Erika Engstrom and Joseph M. Valenzano III.
2014, Lexington Books

Kim Idol, *University of Nevada, Las Vegas*

In their book, *Television, Religion, and* Supernatural: *Hunting Monsters, Finding Gods*, Erika Engstrom and Joseph Valenzano review the popular television series *Supernatural* in terms of the religious and ethical philosophical hierarchies that define its plot and characters, asserting that *Supernatural*, while prioritizing one set of moral values over others, still invites conversation in terms of how particular religions are prioritized (or subordinated) and how this insisted order affects this series' narrative arc.

The authors present *Supernatural* as a discussion of comparative religions, as a presentation of American exceptionalism and as an investigation of patriotism. I in fact disagree with some of the conclusions this work supports, but the arguments within are so soundly developed that I feel invited into the conversation about their validity. The book covers a wide range of topics while remaining true to its central proposal, and includes with an analysis of the validity of popular culture as a way to discuss moral and cultural beliefs that can be deeply held, but are not often examined. Engstrom and Valenzano contend that because *Supernatural*'s main purpose is entertainment it invites an audience that believes in the ideals that drive these quintessentially American cowboys, Sam and Dean Winchester, to investigate these very standards.

I marked this book up because reading it spawned a number of ideas for papers I wanted to write in response. This book encourages creative and passionate responses because of the generous way in which it tackles critical definitions of religiosity, obedience, honor, self-reliance and community values in its investigation of the vital definitions of Americanism and American religiosity. I would read this book for pleasure, for the way in which it invites its audience to respond and I would also use it in the classroom to teach students how to argue well. It is also ruled by a love of the series and therefore allows a television show the respect not easily won when your topic is a family of demon hunters.

Superheroes on World Screens, Edited by Rayna Denison and Rachel Mizsei-Ward, 2015, University Press of Mississippi

Jaq Greenspon, *University of Nevada, Las Vegas*

In 1939, with the introduction of Superman in Action Comics #1, the world changed. While "superheroes" had existed before this, the creation of Siegel and Shuster really put the idea of super powered individuals into the world consciousness. From the beginning, too, there was something global about the comics these characters inhabited. Superman was from a different planet and Captain America, who debuted less than a year later, was shown on the cover of his first issue punching Hitler in the jaw. And yet, both were distinctly "American." Cap had it in his name, and Supes, well, his tag-line was that he fought for "truth, justice, and the American way."

Today, with comic-book heroes becoming multi-billion dollar multi-media properties, it seems the US is no longer big enough to contain these multitudes. This is where the new collection of essays, *Superheroes on World Screens*, comes into the picture. Co-editors (and contributors) Rayna Denison and Rachel Mizsei-Ward have assembled nine diverse pieces on the globalization of the superhero genre. Taken as a whole, the essays paint an interesting picture of global superhero culture, from the sunny streets of San Diego to the crowded inner-city of Thailand. Individually, as with all collections, there are some hits and some misses.

The first section, subtitled "Rethinking the 'Americanness' of US Superheroes," is the most accessible and yet probably the weakest in terms of overall analytic content. This isn't to say they are bad pieces, mind you, just not terribly deep. Kevin Patrick's "The Transplanted Superhero," for instance, looks at the history of Lee Falk's character *The Phantom* in terms of its relationship to Australian popular culture. This is a piece of writing which could easily find a home on one of the many websites featuring comic book history and lore, which I personally appreciate, but lacks the critical eye and academic prose found in many of the other pieces.

The second piece in this section, "Thor, God of Borders," also stretches its point, making too much of the international subcontractors and multi-national cast before acknowledging the film's obvious US sensibilities. While the piece is interesting, author Vincent M. Gaine is trying too hard to fit his ideas into the paradigm required by the book's premise.

Once we get to the third piece, "American Superheroes in Japanese Hands," the work really starts coming into focus, and we get the kind of analysis this book seems to demand of its contributors. Co-editor Denison looks at the Marvel Comics figure Spider-man and how the Japanese culture has not merely replicated the character with their *Supaidāman* but has made him their own. She writes: "What *Supaidāman* reveals, therefore, is the flexibility of the superhero genre, and the ease with which local variations on superheroes can incorporate the early US characters that once offered them inspiration." Additionally, she gets the name of the American hero correct, with the hyphen, something which gets missed in later chapters that mention him.

The next two sections, "Superheroes on World Screens: *From Local Productions to Transnational Blockbusters*" and "The Politics, Morality, and Socio-Cultural Impact of Superheroes on World Screens," both generally bring the academic back to the forefront. Even Chapter 4, "Heroes of Hall H," with its focus on Comic-Con International in general and Doctor Who in particular, is still able to bring a critical eye to the proceedings. The remaining five chapters each take as focus a specific country, using that culture as a lens through which to view the superhero phenomenon, especially in how it relates *back* to the United States.

For example, Daniel Martin's piece about *Blade of the Phantom Master* points out that "one of the most enduring debates taking place within academic studies of Japanese animation is the extent to which it reflects a sense of Japanese-ness. Some critics regard anime as essentially stateless, while others view the recognizably foreign qualities of anime as key to its international appeal." At the same time, in "*Tu Mera Superman*" Iain Robert Smith looks at the qualities of an Indian version of the prototypical hero and how his acquisition of powers, while the same in ability, come from a much more culturally appropriate source (in this case, the Hindu monkey god Hanuman).

The only really disappointing piece is co-editor Ward's contribution "Fighting for Truth, Justice, and the Islamic Way." While discussing the comic and subsequent animated TV series centering around the Islamic-based hero group *The 99*, she is slightly disingenuous in her presentation of data. While she discusses the trouble the show had finding a US broadcasting home in 2010 due to conservative bloggers, she only mentions in a footnote the show's eventual airing via Netflix a mere 2 years later, 3 years before the publication date of this book. Additionally, she postulates the blogging effort to keep the show off American airwaves "may be an aberration" when she cites another show (*Burka Avenger*) with similar characteristics that has not received any notice at all from those same conservative bloggers. However, it isn't until the end of that paragraph she concedes that while the *Burka Avenger* is widely available on the Internet and smartphones, "it has only been aired in Pakistan and has not yet tried to penetrate the US market."

Overall, considering the future worldwide film release schedule of superhero films, this book is a good start at looking at the impact superheroes are having on global culture.

"A Word-Slinger's Delight":
Morrissey's *Autobiography*

Michael A Young, *Independent Scholar*

The autobiography of Steven Patrick Morrissey, singer-songwriter and former frontman of 1980s British band the Smiths, has been much publicised, much hyped, much sold, much praised, much vilified and, perhaps hyperbolically, published as an instant Penguin Classic.[1] So much fuss over a celebrity autobiography written by a popular vocalist and songwriter past the zenith of his 1980s fame prompts the question: What is the book actually like? *Autobiography* is a somewhat unselfcritical, overlong gush of memory, experience and emotion, which nevertheless succeeds both as a source of information about topics larger than its author—the North, particularly in the 1960s and '70s, popular music, the nature of those Siamese twins success and failure—and as a translation of life into language that sometimes delights with its originality and vivid linguistic imagination. If the book has faults typical of celebrity autobiography—an excess of trivia and fascination with the self and its obsessions—it is still generally worth the effort of reading.

Autobiography is partly a story of origins, of Irish immigration and growing up "in forgotten Victorian knife-plunging Manchester" with its "derelict shoulder-to-shoulder houses" (3). Working-class life in the 1960s is very limited: "no one we know is on the electoral roll and a journey by car is as unusual as space travel" (4). Hyperbole, a staple of Morrissey's style, makes the point: "Manchester is a barbaric place where only headless savages can survive" (116). Manchester, a centre of the Industrial Revolution, is classic territory for such a judgment, one that has a long history, going back at least to Engels's *Condition of the Working Class in England* (1845). Morrissey's version of the city is the other end of that history. Perhaps the most vivid focus of this first part of *Autobiography* is the author's school experience: the grim Victorian buildings unfit for purpose, warehouses for the secondary-modern rejects, those who failed the notorious eleven-plus exam and were consigned to the scrapheap before their teens, and the even grimmer teachers indulging their frustration and pathology in violence against the students. The picture should be familiar to any male processed through the state-school system in that period. Overall, the portrait of northern, urban working-class life of that time, with its "aura of making-do" (130), is well drawn and certainly recognisable to those who lived through it. Unfortunately, it is probably familiar to younger generations today: the poverty, the limited educational opportunities or education that leads back where you came from, the frustration of ambition, the sense that a better life lies elsewhere. All of these are still relevant in a North that currently has substantial unemployment and food banks as a growing presence. Elements in *Autobiography* with its vision of a nation divided along class, economic and geographical lines, and the author's awareness "of the disregard London pays to the north" (197), make it not just a personal account but in part a modern and contemporary Condition-of-England text.

Nature, rarely accessible, offers little respite from this grim urban environment but complements and even exceeds it. The dominant version of nature in *Autobiography* is very much a northern one and its epitome is Saddleworth Moor, partly within Greater Manchester and notorious as the burial site of the working-class child victims of Ian Brady and Myra Hindley, the "Moors Murderers," at their hideous work of kidnap, sexual torture and killing from 1963 to '65. The moor is a stereotype of northern nature and described memorably as "at the end of everything" (232). The Brady-Hindley murders give it a ghastly presence and, as a former working-class Manchester lad, Morrissey remembers those crimes, and that one of the victims remains buried on the moor. He has already written and sung about these victims in "Suffer Little Children." In *Autobiography*, a later, Gothic episode (229-39) conjures them again and, distantly, Emily Brontë. In *Wuthering Heights* moorland darkness is embodied as a romantic figure who can be translated into lover and social victim, the excluded Irishman, say, as in Terry Eagleton's reading of that text (Novel 125), or a literal black man, as in Andrea Arnold's recent film version. In *Autobiography*, however, the darkness is both urban and natural, a dangerous, predatory environment whether town or country, not Brontë's ambivalently desirable wildness nor Lawrence's or Ted Hughes's healing, life-giving, though also death-dealing, nature.

Typically for a young person in the North of Morrissey's youth, and probably now, music is seen as an escape: "We gotta get out of this place," as Eric Burdon and the Animals, a northern band from Tyneside, sang in the 1960s. Morrissey claims that "Song [. . .] permitted expressions that otherwise had no way through" (41). He conveys well the excitement of new singles and their origin in a wider world. Most people from pre-CD, pre-download generations will remember that excitement, the pleasure of the smell of warm vinyl, the obsession of playing a new single over and over until it was part of the soundtrack to your life. But Morrissey means more than this: "If I can sing, I am free" (45). Music is an opportunity for creativity, a popular culture in which the otherwise alienated and disenfranchised young can participate actively, an art that transcends the future intended for secondary-modern kids. Individual liberation forms part of wider social shifts: "This feared raggle-clatter of pop species is changing everything" (67-68). Popular music and its performers are altering language, class and gender. Revolutions on the turntable are revolutionising society. Maybe, but the fundamentals of economics and the class system, of the North-South divide which Morrissey describes well, have remained in place. As TV current affairs programmes frequently tell us, we still have a society in which 1% of the population owns 25% of the wealth, and some of that 1% have had a career in popular music. Revolutionary change takes longer than a three-minute single and individual escape from narrow circumstances is not mass liberation. In their powerful revision of the national anthem, the Sex Pistols' refrain of "No future, no future, no future for you" is, unfortunately, still relevant to the social and economic landscape of the North.

In his comments on music, Morrissey lists performers that he found liberating: T Rex, Bowie, Roxy Music, his beloved New York Dolls, Mott the Hoople, Iggy Pop, Lou Reed and Patti Smith (65ff, 114). When Morrissey claims of the last three that "Their contribution to thought marks them out as our very own Goethe, Gide and Gertrude Stein" (114), an eclectic trio, we recognise the hyperbole of both the lover of popular music and the autodidact. Morrissey's overestimate of admired performers shows in his claim that "The arts translate life into film and literature and music and repeat a deadly poison: *the monotonous in life must be protected at all costs.* / But protected from what? / From you and I" (137). As this quotation shows, Morrissey seems to have a chronic problem with the case of the first-person pronoun after a preposition. The pronoun takes the object case, Steven: "From you and *me.*" But it is not only the grammar that is wrong here. The larger and more important point is that the arts as critical comment on and subversion of the established social and moral order did not begin with the New York Dolls. Hyperbole may compel attention but not necessarily agreement.

Despite the centrality of music to Morrissey's life and career, *Autobiography* gives only limited information about his own work. There are general comments on recording sessions, dates of releases, chart positions and sales figures, but these are mostly external aspects of the music. There is no extended comment on the music itself, an omission which may disappoint its fans. Perhaps Morrissey could write a preferably slimmer volume that would discuss his music, tying it back to experiences described in *Autobiography*, though not reducing the songs to what Hopps, rejecting the approach, calls "coded biography" (90).

One thing Morrissey does tell us about music is his experience of the industry and the problems success in it brings. *Autobiography* is good on the trials and travails of the artist in his struggle with popular music as a business: the unfavourable contracts, the lack of both artistic and commercial acumen by record labels and the dearth of talent for production. Informing the reader about such difficulties involves score-settling, more debit than credit, an activity which is a staple of most autobiographies and certainly of Morrissey's. He demolishes everyone from pop fleas like Neil Aspinall (379), through minor figures like the DJ John Peel (157-58) and Sandie Shaw (164-65) to those more closely involved in Morrissey's career, such as Geoff Travis, boss of the Rough Trade label to which the Smiths signed (152ff). Most of these portraits are hatchet jobs, some of them merely dismissive, others very funny. In fact, throughout *Autobiography*, Morrissey indulges in verbal knife-plunging, stabbing everyone from his old school-teachers to Margaret Thatcher (143-44, 226-27) who, according to one study of Morrissey and his music, was a "negative inspiration" (Hopps 28) for him. In most cases, Morrissey's targets seem to deserve the attack, although of course their autobiographies would no doubt give a different version of events.

As for the music industry, its "gluttonous snakes-and-ladders legalities" (170) reach their acme, or nadir, in the notorious 1996 Smiths' trial, in which Michael Joyce, former drummer with the Smiths, brought a civil action against Morrissey for a share of royalties and other income the band supposedly had. Morrissey describes Joyce as "a flea in search of a dog" (302) and gives a long, even overlong, account of the legal hearing, its final judgment and appeal, all of which Morrissey lost. Many long paragraphs in this section testify to the torrent of emotion and commitment to righting the record, a performance not to be interrupted by pause or change of subtopic until the current one is exhausted, though the stark brevity of the author's equation, "fame=money=lawsuits" (321), is convincing. Post-breakup legal actions among former band members are almost a required element of the pop-rock career and part of a long tradition—Pete Best and the Beatles provide an early example—but the Smiths' case is a particularly bitter and, it seems, unjust one, forming a caution against that other staple of a pop-rock career: attending to music but not to business.

When a pre-fame Morrissey submits a script to the TV soap *Coronation Street*, "the twice-weekly crawl through northern morals," he describes his effort as "a word-slinger's delight" (122). The phrase, with its implication of both pleasure and haste in language, applies well to the style and structure of *Autobiography*. The problems and advantages of the style come from the same source. The language tumbles out in a rush of energy, the words propelled by the writer's need to tell his version of the truth. The style is an oral one with the speaker addressing his audience very directly, confessing his anger, frustrations, desires and pleasures. *Autobiography* is a performance in a vocalist's and songwriter's voice. This almost physical first-person style makes immediate contact with its audience and reads quickly, an advantage for such a long book. Sometimes, though, the prose trips over itself to fall into at least minor incoherence and grammatical error. Then the style resembles rush writing with a touch of Tourette's. It's not clear what editing process the text has gone through. Perhaps a desire, author's or publisher's, for the authentic voice has minimised editing, but careful proofing would have reduced these problems while retaining the style's energy and momentum.

Autobiography's opening lines, perhaps a more appropriate term than sentences, give some sense of this style: "My childhood is streets upon streets upon streets upon streets. Streets to define you and streets to confine you, with no sign of motorway, freeway or highway" (3). The rhythm and rhyme of song are audible here and Morrissey has already written and sung about such streets in "Panic." Not surprisingly, some of the book's most graphic writing describes these scenes of Morrissey's urban childhood, an environment that persists at least into the 1980s: "Manchester's most pickled poor live in these surrounds—non-human sewer rats with missing eyes; the loudly insane with indecipherable speech patterns; the mad poor of Manchester's armpit" (138). In Morrissey's youth the tramps wear "clothes brewing with meth-stench" (25) and his father is "fist-ready with the outside world" (22). Morrissey's descriptions of "the slate-landscape of out-of-time Lancashire. An eternity of repetitive streets of Victorian terraced houses" (107) are reminiscent of Jeanette Winterson's writing about Accrington's "stretchy" (85) streets. Generally, the urban North prompts the best writing in *Autobiography*. There are, however, other instances of vivid language, even if these are sometimes set in overlong, prosaic passages. Morrissey's answer to an accusation of grammatical error in a song's lyrics is a good example: "'Yessssssssssssssss,' I hiss, like an adder on heat, *'it's meant to be there'*" (216). The simile perfectly doubles the affirmative's sibilant tail of fifteen s's, a visual and aural conjuring of the snake itself. If admiration is instantly displaced by amusement with the completion of the sentence, "and *now* I know how Joan of Arc felt" (216), this simply indicates the mixed quality of the text, its frequent resort to hyperbole and the consistency of Morrissey's references, since in the song "Bigmouth Strikes Again," Morrissey compares himself to Joan of Arc. Yet the gift of language, a genuine feeling for it, in that wonderful German term, *Sprachgefühl*, is definitely there throughout *Autobiography*, even if only sporadically.

The structure of *Autobiography* parallels the style and displays the same faults and virtues. Overall, the structure is episodic, picaresque, with a forward chronological movement through the different stages of the author's experience. Within these, there is a rush of jump-cuts, anecdotes and digressions, a tumble of bits and pieces building to the retrospective coherence we call a life. In one paragraph, for example, we go from pop music to football to failing the eleven-plus to secondary education and back to pop (54). Somehow, the paragraph works, because it re-enacts life as we experience it and recaptures an immediacy of thought and feeling. The paragraph is a microcosm of the text's larger structure where the lack of transitions obligatory in a more formal style and structure reproduces the jumble of actual experience and spoken language. Often, this loose, orally based structure suits the content. Throughout the latter part of *Autobiography*, for example, there are snapshots of various celebrities presented in a kind of *paparazzi* structure. This works, since it accurately reproduces the bounce of quick contact in these encounters. Yet these structural choices sometimes impose limitations. At one point, Morrissey is in Paris for half a page and then suddenly, without any transition other than a paragraph division with a missing first-line indent, he is in Halifax and Leeds (391-92). Such lack of formally marked structure may reproduce the confused and jolting rush of celebrity existence, life as a tour itinerary, but may also disorient the reader. Confetti is not a sustainable model for extended narrative structure or substantial, coherent comment on a topic.

In a reflection of the essential ordinariness of the protagonists and their lives, celebrity memoirs, usually ghost-written, are mostly tedious and vacuous. Morrissey's effort is much better than the ruck of such volumes. In language that is sometimes vivid, he gives a graphic picture of northern, working-class life in the 1960s and'70s, the evils of the school system of that time and place, some good, quick portraits of people, the difficulties of the music business, a sense of the arbitrariness of the legal system and the risks that attend success. On the other hand, one of these risks is self-absorption, perhaps inevitably magnified in the writing of one's life story, and Morrissey does not totally avoid this problem. In the last part of the book particularly, a naturally hyperbolic style combines with a playlist of concerts barely salvaged from tedium by flashes of writing ability. By the end of this somewhat overweight volume, many readers will have had enough of the superficial minutiae of the celebrity life, the adolescent politics and the obsession with animal protectionism. And yet, A. A. Gill's Hatchet Job of the Year notwithstanding, any text that offers a phrase such as "forgotten Victorian knife-plunging Manchester" (3) is worth the effort, maybe even 457 pages of it.

Notes

[1] At the date of completing this essay, 14 May 2014, there were 379 customer reviews of *Autobiography* on amazon.co.uk for the paperback edition alone. No less an academic luminary than Terry Eagleton has written interestingly about the book in the *Guardian*'s Review Section, while the same issue lists *Autobiography* as number one paperback non-fiction bestseller, with 10,348 copies sold in the UK that week ("Weekly Charts" 21). Published as late in the year as October, the paperback edition still managed to achieve number forty-seven in the bestsellers list for 2013, with total sales of 140,729 copies (Dugdale 16). Autobiography was the first book recommended in the music part of the *Guardian* Review Section's "Christmas Books: The Best of 2013" issue (Lynskey 9).

Perhaps the best-known response to the book is A. A. Gill's review, originally published in the *Sunday Times* and winner of *The Omnivore*'s Hatchet Job of the Year award, "an annual celebration of unkind book reviewing" (Clark

21). Gill's review, a mandarin sneer not only at Morrissey but at popular culture in general, particularly music, is hilarious but only partly deserved. Eagleton's review is much more balanced.

Works Cited

The Animals. "We Gotta Get Out of This Place." Columbia, 1965. Vinyl.

Clark, Alex. "Spiteful, Snarling Reviews." *Guardian* 15 Feb. 2014, Review Section: 9. Print.

Dugdale, John. "Bestsellers 2013." *Guardian* 28 Dec. 2013, Review Section: 16-17. Print.

Eagleton, Terry. *The English Novel*. Oxford: Blackwell, 2005. Print.

---. "Shyness + Vitriol." Rev. of *Autobiography*, by Morrissey. *Guardian* 16 Nov. 2013, Review Section: 9. Print.

Engels, Frederick. *The Condition of the Working Class in England*. 1845. London: Lawrence and Wishart, 1973. Print.

Gill, A. A. "A Martyr to Himself." Rev. of *Autobiography*, by Morrissey. *Sunday Times* 27 Oct. 2013, Culture Section: 37-38. "A. A. Gill on *Autobiography* by Morrissey." *The Omnivore*. Web. 20 Feb. 2014.

Hopps, Gavin. *Morrissey: The Pageant of His Bleeding Heart*. New York: Continuum, 2009.

Lynskey, Dorian. "Get into the Groove." *Guardian* 7 Dec. 2013, Review Section: 9. Print.

Morrissey. *Autobiography*. London: Penguin, 2013. Print.

The Sex Pistols. "God Save the Queen." Virgin, 1977. Vinyl.

The Smiths. "Bigmouth Strikes Again." *The Queen Is Dead*. Rough Trade, 1986. LP.

---. "Panic." Rough Trade, 1986. Single.

---. "Suffer Little Children." *The Smiths*. Rough Trade, 1984. LP.

"The Weekly Charts." *Guardian* 16 Nov. 2013, Review Section: 21. Print.

Winterson, Jeanette. *Why Be Happy When You Could Be Normal?* London: Cape, 2011. Print.

Wuthering Heights. Dir. Andrea Arnold. Artificial Eye, 2011. Film.

Popular Culture Review, the refereed journal of the Far West Popular and American Culture Associations, is published twice yearly by Westphalia Press and widely indexed in sources including the MLA Bibliography. Subscriptions are included as part of membership in FWPCA/FWACA.

One need not be a member to submit an article for consideration but must join the organization on acceptance. Queries about membership and articles for consideration should be sent to felicia.campbell@unlv.edu.

The journal invites articles on all aspects of popular culture worldwide as well as on American culture.

Popular Culture Review gratefully acknowledges the contributions and support by the UNLV College of Liberal Arts and the UNLV Department of English.

Articles published do not necessarily represent the opinions of and are not the legal responsibility of *Popular Culture Review*.

ISSN 1060-8125

FWPCA/ACA 28th Annual Meeting, February 26 – 28, 2016
Palace Station Hotel, Las Vegas

Call for Papers

Now accepting papers on all aspects of Popular Culture worldwide and American Culture. Send abstracts of 50 to 75 words to felicia.campbell@unlv.edu before December 15, 2015. Please include your affiliation, if any, and a postal mailing address. We encourage early submissions. Visit us at fwpca.org, and please "Like" *Far West PCA* on Facebook.

www.ingramcontent.com/pod-product-compliance
Lightning Source LLC
Chambersburg PA
CBHW060516280326
41933CB00014B/2994